"Here we have one of the best Christian writers of our time reflecting on one of the best Christians of our time, or any time. Bill has a rare, gentle thoughtfulness and insight that helps us unpack the profound word and witness of Daniel Berrigan. I hope this book inspires many to study Dan's life and writings anew and to deepen our own witness to peace and nonviolence, that we might become, like Daniel Berrigan, disciples, apostles, and prophets of the nonviolent Jesus to our broken world."

—**John Dear**, editor of *Daniel Berrigan: Essential Writings*

"In these relentlessly compelling pages, Dan Berrigan keeps coming at us. We get Dan's wisdom, courage, passion, honesty, good humor, faith, joy, and eloquent gracefulness. And besides all of that, we get the imagery and testimony of his wide circle of friends who shared his passionate vocation of justice. We get all of this because of the generous gifts of Bill Wylie-Kellermann, gifts of poetic cadence, good memory, strong imagination, a close friendship with Dan, and a passion for justice not unlike that of Berrigan himself. This deeply moving book consists in poems, memories, sermons, speeches, and testimonies that will keep Dan's singular legacy alive for time to come. The book is a welcome gift to us. It is indeed compelling in ways that will both unnerve and give nerve to an attentive reader."

—**Walter Brueggemann**, Columbia Theological Seminary

"Beneath all the lives of the saints there lies the mycelium of friendship. In *Celebrant's Flame*, Wylie-Kellermann orates Daniel Berrigan's sacred story. Yes, as Catholic priest, social prophet, and liturgical poet, but first and foremost, as friend. Wylie-Kellermann's intimate and wry turn of phrase allows their holy friendship to again do its alchemical work: transforming readers of the Word into its creative witnesses."

—**Rose Marie Berger**, senior editor at *Sojourners* and author of *Bending the Arch*

"Daniel Berrigan's death in 2016 meant the loss of one of the greatest prophetic voices in the history of US Catholicism. Bill's book helps us to heed that voice anew. In addition to presenting an intimate portrait of Berrigan's witness, Bill's own experience uniquely illuminates the vibrant world of radical Christian activism from the latter twentieth century to now, populated with a wide cast of characters. Reader beware: you might become one yourself!"

—**Dean Dettloff**, lecturer, Institute for Christian Studies

"The clear-sightedness of this stunning book is life-sustaining: root yourself in the gospel, find your community and dwell there, love one another, and act on the side of life—always! Those steeped in Daniel Berrigan's writings and life will be delighted with Wylie-Kellermann's deft ability to engage and renew Berrigan's familiar work while also opening paths to anti-racist solidarity, climate justice, and COVID-19 mutual aid work. This book breathed life into the dried bones of America and my own. Wylie-Kellermann knows the rocky ground we must tread, but he also knows we must be people of the resurrection."

—**Anna J. Brown**, coeditor and author of *Faith, Resistance, and the Future: Daniel Berrigan's Challenge to Catholic Social Thought*

"In this homage to, and multifaceted portrait of, his beloved friend and mentor, Wylie-Kellermann exhumes old correspondence, excavates forgotten files and re-members community mementos from a movement that spiritually and politically birthed him (and me, and so many others). This is a kind of family scrapbook, rich with loving marginal notes (Bill's and others), dog-eared clippings, and poignant snapshots of a consequential life. Through his vintage poetic prose, Wylie-Kellermann offers a treasure trove of sacred story, testimony, and memory to all who were midwifed to gospel faith by Dan Berrigan—and to our spiritual progeny."

—**Ched Myers**, coauthor of *Ambassadors of Reconciliation and Healing Haunted Histories: A Settler Discipleship of Decolonization*

Celebrant's Flame

Celebrant's Flame

Daniel Berrigan in Memory and Reflection

Bill Wylie-Kellermann

FOREWORD BY
Frida Berrigan

AFTERWORD BY
Kateri Boucher

 CASCADE *Books* • Eugene, Oregon

Cascade Books
An Imprint of Wipf and Stock Publishers
199 W. 8th Ave., Suite 3
Eugene, OR 97401

www.wipfandstock.com

PAPERBACK ISBN: 978-1-6667-0189-0
HARDCOVER ISBN: 978-1-6667-0190-6
EBOOK ISBN: 978-1-6667-0191-3

Cataloguing-in-Publication data:

Names: Wylie-Kellermann, Bill, author. | Berrigan, Frida, foreword. | Boucher, Kateri, afterword.

Title: Celebrant's flame : Daniel Berrigan in memory and reflection / by Bill Wylie-Kellermann ; foreword by Frida Berrigan ; afterword by Kateri Boucher.

Description: Eugene, OR: Cascade Books, 2021 | Includes bibliographical references.

Identifiers: ISBN 978-1-6667-0189-0 (paperback) | ISBN 978-1-6667-0190-6 (hardcover) | ISBN 978-1-6667-0191-3 (ebook)

Subjects: LCSH: Berrigan, Daniel, 1921–2016. | Catholic Church—United States—Catholic Clergy—Biography. | Pacifists—United States—Biography.

Classification: BX4705.B3845 W5 2021 (print) | BX4705 (ebook)

All quotes from Daniel Berrigan are used with permission from the Daniel Berrigan Literary Trust.

04/07/21

For Clare Grady
(indeed, the greater Grady clan)
with Elizabeth McAlister
and all of the Kings Bay Plowshares
for enacting, like Daniel and Philip,
their own hammer-rung witness
of love

Giving Voice

(for Daniel Berrigan on his birthday)

the heart dares the word dares the page
lest love stick in the throat of this pen,
and go untold

I remember my name
in your voice
echoing down the underground hall
beneath Niebuhr Place:
come, crack a jar of scotch
come for talk and a minted brew of tea
come to life. wake. arise.
(an ascent follows, sweet and rash)

somehow that calling
pipes through the Kentucky hills retreat.
while I practiced sport, before smoke rose from Detroit
your prayer with Merton and circle
breached the walls to fall also on me.
summoning unbeknownst an answer.

(later, in a season of crushing dark
you opened for me the gatehouse door
there to walk and breathe and eat the psaltery
to face dread dreams and heal)

confess a thing:
even on this island now
the tabletalk of poet and keeper
hatches the seminary renegade.
that heady charismatic anarchy
revives as we speak
and our once fresh formation
turns, can it be, toward eldering.

as toward the body politic
body of word presented,
burning with truth the charnel house lies,
this blood on pillars, a gash of vermillion,
or hammering word at the door of church and state.
in consequence, this bravery with a difference
the holy ghost gone militant
free in the cuff, in the dock, in the yard

for all
for missives kited in and out
for the discipline of hope
for drinking the moon underground
for writing on the wall, against it
for bread in lotus fingers

all echoes in the heart at dusk
footfalls on the way beloved

this thanks untellable

Contents

CONTENTS

Acknowledgments

Big thanks of my heart . . .

To Daniel Berrigan for being no less, but also no more, than himself—one in all the marvelous intersections of his whoness. And for uttering my own call to discipleship.

To Kateri Boucher for receiving, in the name of a new generation, the flame of a Berrigan torch through her thoughtful afterword and for being my quiet collaborator in this book.

To Frida Berrigan for naming gentleness, friendship, and wisdom as the need of this moment and for finding them in the pages of the book. Her foreword is a great gift.

To John Bach, Kathy Kelly, Eric Martin, and Jim Reale for personal letters to me about Dan as I wrote. And for their permission to include them here, adding another layer of love and community to this testimony.

To artist and graphic novelist Dylan Meconis (https://www.dylanmeconis. com/) for her iconic poster of Dan which she has lent for a cover. Beauty of thought and line. Two sweet providences: "celebrant's flame" is actually from the very Berrigan poem that he proffers as a scroll—a portion of "Tulips in the Prison Yard." On the occasion of Dan's death, she painted it for her father, Charles Meconis, who was part of our class with Dan at Woodstock/Union in New York, 1973!

To John Dear, Daniel Berrigan's friend and literary executor, for setting this book in motion by inviting me into a related project, for encouraging it vociferously, and for generously granting carte blanche permission to use Dan's letters, poems, speeches, quips, and book quotations.

To Michael Murphy for offering an equally sweeping permission: "Bill Wylie-Kellermann is empowered to publish, in any form and at any time, any paper or talk he has given or will give in the future for the The Hank Center for the Catholic Intellectual Heritage at Loyola University Chicago."

To Jim Forest for writing so deftly the wonderful biography and memoir of Dan, *At Play in the Lion's Den* (I've had it close at hand and cite it throughout) and for permission to use herein passages from that book, as well as "Contemplation and Resistance: A Conversation Between Nhat Hanh and Daniel Berrigan," from WIN magazine, 1973. Another sweeping generosity: "Any text that I have control of you are welcome to use."

To Jeanie Wylie and *The Witness* magazine, which she edited, for capturing and publishing Dan's story "A Celtic Passage."

To Lydia Wylie-Kellermann for the wisdom and confidence she has offered, and for permission to adapt two articles from *Geez* (https://geez magazine.org/), of which she is editor: "Eucharist at Gunpoint," Issue 56, Spring 2020 and "Daniel Berrigan: Incarnating Poetics of Resistance," issue 53, Spring 2019.

To Satori Shakuur and The Secret Society of Twisted Storytellers, for permission to use "We Shall Not be Moved: Words Won't Make it Happen," March 21, 2014—Charles Wright Museum of African American History, Detroit.

To Eric Martin for his remarkable dissertation, *A Theology of Disobedience: The Conversion of Daniel Berrigan 1953–1966*, Fordham University, New York, June 2019, and for permission to quote it. In my own section on Dan and Phil in the Freedom Struggle, I have relied so heavily on his chapter "I Came on Another Way: The Civil Rights Movement, 1957–1963" that he is all but a collaborator.

ACKNOWLEDGMENTS

To Amanda Daloisio and *The Catholic Worker*, though anarchist and uncopyrighted, for welcoming the reprint of a review on *The Berrigan Letters*, and an adaptation of a review essay on Camus's *The Plague*, to a longer chapter.

To *Sojourners* magazine for two articles, one reprinted, "An Unbound Spirit" from the November 2018 issue, and another adapted, "We Die Before We Live" from the August 2016 issue. Reprinted with permission from *Sojourners*, (800) 714-7474, www.sojo.net.

To *CrossCurrents* for licensing to me as author, "Death Shall Have No Dominion: Daniel Berrigan of the Resurrection," September, 2016. Adapted herein.

To New Directions for lines from "The Moslems' Angel of Death" by Thomas Merton, from THE COLLECTED POEMS OF THOMAS MERTON, copyright ©1963 by The Abbey of Gethsemani. Reprinted by permission of New Directions Publishing Corp.

To friends who read and commented on portions of the manuscript: Terrance Moran, Kathy Kelly, Alana Alpert, John Bach, Frida Berrigan, Kateri Boucher, John Dear, Denise Griebler, Patrick Henry, Michael Lerner, Jeanne Magnotti Randels, Eric Martin, Bob Randels, Jim Reale, Kim Redigan, Justin Sledge, Arthur Waskow, Lucia Wylie-Eggart, Lydia Wylie-Kellermann, and Cat Zettner

To Cascade Books for publishing, and especially to my editor, Rodney Clapp, for encouragement, care, and detail.

To Denise Griebler for permission to name her here as lover, listener, and COVID podmate, and for being my reader, first and fullmost, great thanks and love.

Foreword

Frida Berrigan

WHERE IS THE PLACE for gentleness, the quiet strength that suffers no fools, but envelops them in a transformative embrace? This was my plaintive and panicked question as an armed insurrectionary mob hammered through the doors of the Capitol, hoarse and frenzied in their bloodlust. It reverberates now; I can't stop asking it.

Where is the place for Wisdom, may her name be blessed? This question comes even as my own attention span shrinks to the size of a single pixel and I grasp for easy answers and quick fixes or sink into a squirrel-like collection of information. Phil Berrigan was fond of quoting Martin Luther King's warning about the "paralysis of analysis," which mired friends and community in an endless holding pattern of "what about?" and "what if?" Wisdom is the patience to discern, the discipline to hear and heed the still small voice of conscience and the courage to allow it to blossom into the confidence to act. Where is Wisdom at? We need her right now!

Where is the place for friendship, the balm and motivation, that deep and abiding love, the *what for* of it all? In this COVID age, I am often alone, bereft of friends, heedless of others, plowing through public space, masked and bundled. I am torn between my desire to connect and my fear of contagion. When I do connect with friends, it is unsatisfying and incomplete—a masked encounter where everyone is talking too loud.

Bill wrote *Celebrant's Flame* in the crucible of the conjoined pandemics of coronavirus and white racism and hatred unmasked. In this strange time, the world shrank to four walls and the family unit, but it got a heck of a lot louder and harsher and many of us were tempted—are tempted—to just pull up the covers and give in to despair.

Into that breach, into that tear in our fabric of human connections, comes this timeless chronicle of gentleness, wisdom, and friendship. Insistent and steady, a balm and a nudge, a necessary reminder that all that is required of us—*all* that is required of *us*—is a collective inhale and exhale—conspiracy, connection, courage.

Bill's book and Dan's life, and their lives intertwined and woven with so many others—including mine—remind me that while this hard and protracted moment is unique, it is not new. The principalities of power, racism, and war-making endure. They change form and face, but they are what we are up against. Thankfully, the resources we have are also enduring—gentleness, wisdom, and friendship. They don't seem like enough to work with, but they are!

One of the graces of COVID's rupture of normality has been Zoom *lectio divina* with my mother, Liz McAlister, and a small group of friends. We chat until my mother's subtle expressions of impatience move the group to assign readings and take in the word together. We identify a line that speaks to us, share it, and then—in a second go-round—share what that line is saying to us that morning. And we share so much more—hopes and fears, worries and burdens . . . and more laughter than the disciples would have thought appropriate. Once we have all shared, we offer prayers of petition, say the prayer that Jesus taught us, and say goodbye until tomorrow. It usually takes just an hour, but it is an hour that gives meaning and weight and energy to all the rest of the hours.

I often reflect on how many other people are reading the same words as we are, including our friends in prison for the Kings Bay Plowshares witness in Georgia on April 4, 2018—the fiftieth anniversary of Dr. Martin Luther King, Jr.'s assassination. We are all connected! A necessary reminder in these isolating times.

Liz McAlister has dementia and struggles through many tasks that used to be second nature to her. *Lectio divina* with some of her oldest friends is where she reconnects with her essential self. On this awkward platform, she is sagacious and self-reflective, political and emphatic, funny and empathetic. I sit next to her, leaning close to take it all in, struggling to write it all down, half in disbelief that the woman who couldn't find her bathroom ten minutes earlier has everyone in stitches about something Job said two millennia ago.

Gentleness, wisdom, friendship.

It is right here. It is right now.

It is always the right time and right place for gentleness, wisdom, and friendship. And *Celebrant's Flame* calls me back, gives me ballast, repots me in the rich soil needed to nurture the long haul. I hope you'll close this book repotted too.

Frida Berrigan is a writer and wageless worker who lives in New London, Connecticut with her family: an eight-person, two-household community of elder care known (perhaps only to her) as the Moldy Whale. Her parents, Liz McAlister and Philip Berrigan, formed Jonah House as a community of prayer and nonviolent resistance in the 1970s. She is the author of It Runs in the Family: On Being Raised by Radicals and Growing into Rebellious Motherhood *(New York: OR Books, 2014).*

Preface: These Intersections

> Society had developed and perfected a whole lexicon as ways of stigmatizing the wrong that threatened its wrongs. You know the phrases: to the poor—wrong side of the tracks; to a child in school—wrong question, wrong answer; to the people's spectrum—wrong color; to the women—wrong sex; to the gays—wrong ecstasy.—Daniel Berrigan, March 15, 1974, "All Honor to the Wrong People."[1]

IN 1974 THE WAR Resisters League Peace Award was given to Daniel Berrigan. The honor was conscious counternarrative, an audacious act of love and respect. Beat poet Allen Ginsberg was the formal presenter, reading, "To Daniel Berrigan, for his irritating vocation as a prophet in our times, angering us in our complacency, embracing us in our humanity. Leaping beyond his own limits, he has led us beyond ours." In Dan's honor, Ginsberg followed with a long poem, "Jaweh and Allah Battle."[2]

The year prior Berrigan had been invited to address the Association of Arab-American University Graduates in DC. But then the October/Yom Kippur War broke. He kept the date, speaking as the bombs fell. Confessing his own inexpertise, and excoriating all sides of the war for violence (including our own US, and Christian "sides"), he nonetheless came down firm in outraged love for Israel's betrayal of what he read as its own history and tradition—one akin to his own. He did not mince words. A firestorm broke. He was accused of being wrong in every way or other. Invitations were withdrawn, awards cancelled. Hence, WRL's honor and his own words to embrace being wrong.

---

1. D. Berrigan, "All Honor to the Wrong People."
2. Ginsberg, "Jaweh and Allah Battle."

For a variety reasons, and with a short introduction, I've included the entire speech in this volume. I do consider it prophetic. And he paid up personally for the utterance. But I begin with it here for two reasons. One, because some time after, he asked a group of us, seminarians then his students, why we hadn't issued a public statement supporting him. Honestly, it never even occurred to us that we had the agency to weigh in publicly on such a stage. His wounded lament was, in effect, another lesson. Your voice matters. Speak up. Never too late to learn.

A lesser reason is simply the quote above, which it prompted, about the ways and identities of being wrong in this culture. He was naming, in simple and straightforward fashion, a short list of what today would be called intersections of oppression. (Not to mention implicit forms of resistance).

I've organized these reflections around aspects of his identity and vocation. So, prisoner, poet, prophet, priest, and so on—all the facets that were and always will be, of Daniel Berrigan. Some of these bear no ordinary stigma of oppression, though it may be said he suffered for each. And while they may be distinct in discipline or relationship, they all overlap with a certain simultaneity. Hence, John Bach writes about Berrigan as teacher, but the whole episode is set in prison. The section on Dan as prisoner is built around a long poem of his. The chapter on Dan as poet is ultimately about prophetic action. Since his nonviolent action was liturgical, it gets fullest treatment in the chapter on priesthood. Being pastorally present to the dying in hospice is a form of urban contemplation. In such ways and more, these intersections flow in and out of one another in being truly himself.

If you don't know who Daniel Berrigan is, or know just a little, start with chapter 1. Or maybe chapter 9. Otherwise, should you know of him, even perhaps know him well, start where you like. Any section might be a good way in.

I'm mindful that many people could have written a similar book, perhaps better, though it would hardly have been this one. It's fairly personal. Even where I've pulled together material new to myself, it's threaded and vetted by my own memories, history, and love for him. I'm not trying to be objective, at least not trying too hard. Dan changed my life and I hope it shows and shows through. More than once I've fallen into a hole: who the hell am I to write this? It's his voice that calls me out. Sometimes literally, in the lines of old letters.

Incidentally, I should say that John Dear is to blame for this book. (And I don't mean just his exuberant enthusiasm for it more than once.) He called last fall to ask that I write something short on Dan. Just to get my juices flowing I pulled up and printed out a number of things previously written. Laid out before me on the desk, I suddenly asked, Hmm, are these pieces of a book? Ted Lewis and the editors at Cascade quickly answered yes, and here we are. I should add that John previously published a book on Dan, *Apostle of Peace*,[3] which is similarly organized, but in that instance collecting essays on these topics by a variety of prominent people. I can commend it. Let's call this a companion volume.

A number of these essays, I'm happy to say, are brand new. Others are old and spruced up a bit, even one almost fifty years old (I had to transcribe it from a carbon copy, if you know what that is). Consequently, there's necessarily a little repetition you may have to bear with. A friend reading portions referred to the occasional duplications as echoes or refrains. Please take them so.

There are a few other voices. I started out by making space for a letter about Dan, and it happily proliferated to four letters included. A sweet device.

Dan's own voice is prominent in these pages. Three sections are entirely in his own words: a wedding homily, a long poem, and the controversial speech. Plus, snips of letters, poems, and autobiographical musings. They are the best written of the book.

I have, quite conscientiously, not asked, "What would Berrigan do?" in the face of our current deepening nuclear crisis, or the slower incineration of the planet, or the violent re-emergence of long-standing white supremacy, or the hundreds of thousands of COVID deaths and its structured impact on low-income people. To do so would render him a moral cipher, reduce him to some set of principles, even let us off the hook of "What am I to do?" In answering the latter, we can surely be formed and transformed by immersion in his witness. We can learn to live in a sacramental or resurrectional ethic.

I knew him but partially, as all things this side of the veil. I pray these reflections will be a contribution to the fullness of his blessed memory. Above all, I write for a new generation to take him in. Take him up. To that end, I'm so grateful that his niece, Frida Berrigan, first generation, has offered a foreword. And that Kateri Boucher, a young Millennial Catholic

---

3. Dear, ed., *Apostle of Peace*.

Worker who has been my quiet collaborator, has taken up the torch in an afterword. Bless their souls and the light they shed.

Bill Wylie-Kellermann

Martin Luther King, Jr. Day, 2021

— Chapter 1 —

A Life: Reflections on a Biography

WHEN FATHER DANIEL BERRIGAN[1] and his brother Philip, along with A. J. Muste, John Howard Yoder, and a handful of budding Catholic radicals gathered in 1964 with Thomas Merton at Gethsemani Abbey for a retreat concerning the Spiritual Roots of Protest, the intercessions of that meeting, I am convinced, not only seeded a movement, but fell upon me, summoning my vocation.

Four years later when the Berrigan brothers with seven others entered the draft board in Catonsville, Maryland, removed the 1-A files (of those eligible for sending to the Vietnam war front), and burned them with homemade napalm, those ashes too would eventually anoint my life and pastoral calling. Daniel turned that action toward liturgy, toward poetry. He edited the transcript of their conviction in federal court into a play of international repute, refused induction into the prison system, and went notoriously underground for four months, writing and speaking from the "most wanted list" before being captured by the FBI at the Block Island home of his friend William Stringfellow. When he was released after two years in the federal system, Berrigan came to New York City and taught a course on the Apocalypse of St. John when I was a student at Union Seminary. Full disclosure: Dan Berrigan became to me not merely teacher, but a mentor and friend.

In the year following Dan's death at nearly ninety-five (+April 30, 2016+), Jim Forest undertook the heroic literary effort of writing *At Play in the Lion's Den: A Biography and Spiritual Memoir of Daniel Berrigan* (Orbis, 2017). Perhaps he had a running start. Three things are notable about the book up front. One is that Forest's own life and callings are inextricably

---

1. Wylie-Kellermann, first published as "An Unbound Spirit."

1

tangled with Berrigan's. (He was, for example, editor of the *Catholic Worker* when Dan first appeared there, was himself part of the Merton retreat, hatched with Dan and staffed the Catholic Peace Fellowship, and responded to Catonsville with his own participation in a draft board raid joining others in Milwaukee within the year.) So, like the Acts of the Apostles, there are whole sections written in the first-person voice. Other places, he peeks from behind the elegant narrative to lend a knowing detail or simply cites the voices of others with a certainty of having been there too. For a biographer, this is a vested and risky high-wire act. Don't fall into self-aggrandizement (his genuine modesty saves him that) or the net of personal hagiography. And best to confess up front by title: *Biography and Spiritual Memoir*, a difficult art he has mastered.

Another note is that he solicited a circle of collaborators to tell their own testimonies, answer questions, comment, and correct the occasional misplaced assumption. In that sense the book is a veritable act of community. Not so much collectively written as collectively underwritten. Okay, fuller disclosure: I was among those solicited, contributing ever so slightly to the story.

A third concerns photographs. Forest once published a pictorial life of Thomas Merton. When he expanded and republished his biography of Dorothy Day, he filled the book with photos. *At Play in the Lion's Den* shares with each a common editor and publisher, Robert Ellsberg of Orbis Books, and a similar commitment to the visual. Every chapter of text is illuminated with a host of photos. Posters, banner holds, caricatured birthday invites, the *Time* magazine cover of Dan and Phil dragging the church into non-violence by the collar, towering puppets for an underground escape, whole walls of art and loved ones, courtroom sketches, and the inevitable book covers from lauded poetry, to resistance shelf, and finally the biblical commentaries mining Jesus and the prophets. There are photographs of compatriots and conversation partners: Dorothy Day, Merton, Thich Nhat Hanh, Howard Zinn, Ernesto Cardenal, Stringfellow, Eqbal Ahmad, Elizabeth McAlister, Muste, and King, never mind beginning to end—Philip, Philip, Philip. But above all himself, in mother Frida's arms or beneath Dado's scowl, pious and well-scrubbed, pensive, mugshot, chastened or chagrined, exuberant, mid-utterance, the mike or camera in his face, free in the cuffs, the dock, the cell, laughing aloud or just about to. Always it seems there is love in his eye, and somehow free delight.

Like Gandhi's "experiments in truth," Forest tracks moments in Berrigan's conversion to the gospel of nonviolence. To be sure he was raised in a home where the *Catholic Worker* was present, but he didn't seem to be reading it during World War II where in the isolation of seminary, he blessed our soldiers, Philip among them, in their cause for Christ. Post-war, he did create a small dust-up reading *God and the Atom* and sharing it with his first high school charges. A year in France (he came to love the place) moved him forward with exposure to both the "worker priest" movement and the front-page reports of Dien Bien Phu—the collapse of the French war in Vietnam. Back in the states he met Dorothy Day and began a decisive lifelong relationship to her Catholic Worker movement. Knew it or not, his conversion was met in earnest. Add Phil's early experience with racial justice work and conversation with Christians of Eastern Europe, and by the time of the Merton retreat he was in deep conversion.

Prelude to Catonsville was the anti-war self-immolation of the young Catholic Worker, Roger LaPorte. (See Dan's discussion of that with Thich Nhat Hanh in *The Raft is Not the Shore.*[2]) Forest reproduces portions of his memorial homily for the community that actually triggered his ecclesial exile to Latin America, yet another station on the way. In 1968, a more immediate prelude was his night flight to Hanoi with Howard Zinn to retrieve American POWs. There, in a shelter, he tasted life beneath US bombing. Between that and the draft board action was the assassination of Martin King. Find the cost of freedom. God loves a moving target and Berrigan's conversion to gospel nonviolence ran effectively lifelong. The big events, like Catonsville or the 1980 General Electric action (hammering swords/ nuclear delivery vehicles into plowshares) are the ones where the struggle of discernment within the movement was a refiner's fire. Was destruction of property nonviolent? At first, though they eventually affirmed, Dorothy and Merton would have held him back. Phil pulled forward.

In between and thereafter the elements of conversion were perpetual: the network of safehouses built in his underground sojourn; the ragtag study communities gathered in prison; suffering the heatstorm from Israel for his biting critique on behalf of Palestinians; pressing nonviolence with the Weather Underground domestically, and with Ernesto Cardenal in Central America; the endless Pentagon actions—blood and ashes—with Jonah House folk.

2. Berrigan and Nhat Hanh, *Raft.*

My own conversion to gospel nonviolence came at Daniel's hand. Or at his word. Call it the witness of his life. And it precipitated a genuine crisis in me. He served in that period as something of a spiritual director to me and offered cold comfort: "You're getting born and it's bloody. It's always bloody." Don't have to wonder how he knew that. He is so often called prophet or poet or priest, and rightly, but too rarely "apostle or evangelist" of nonviolence.[3] I venture to say that his is a life, even again in the telling, which calls so many of us to radical discipleship. *Deo Gratias.*

---

3. John Dear does. See Dear, ed., *Apostle.*

Transformative Aside: Conversion
(A Letter from Eric Martin)

December 11, 2020

Dear Bill,

It's Winter in America, as Gil Scott-Heron put it, and you ask me to say a word about Dan and transformation. It seems a fitting task, given the circumstances of his life and witness, and a hopeful one, given ours.

I met Dan in his late eighties, when I assumed his transformations would be over. Unlike most who knew him, our tales together are pretty tame. No arrests, no protests, no parties with liquor in the bathtub, no liturgies of questionable orthodoxy. We only ventured outdoors once in all our time together. He already lived on Thompson Street, meaning the only time I entered the famed 98th St. Jesuit community where he used to reside was to celebrate its final community dinner before closing. His body too seemed on the verge of closing its doors, a reality which definitively framed my visits to his armchair, then his wheelchair, and, eventually, his bedside.

I wrote him a letter from a pit of confusion, as I later learned so many others had before. Would he be willing to call this stranger to talk? "Of course, and come for tea," he bade. Forget the phone.

Our long sit continues to transform my life. A vocational path that seemed morally closed became, in his zen hands, reopened, vivified, blessed. More importantly, he gave me an address. A Catholic-become-atheist-become-Catholic-again in my early twenties, I felt lost in the Church, as if it had no space for me or my ultimate concerns. He heard this, held it, consulted a notebook, and copied for me "503 Rock Creek Church Rd NW." When I later looked quizzically at the "Catholic Worker" sign outside this DC house as a tall man named Art Laffin opened the door, I remembered Dan's assurance: "You'll find your people there." I did, and do.

When I eventually started the PhD in theology that Dan cleared a way for, he moved to the retirement home on the edge of campus, just a two-minute walk from my classes. I landed up writing my dissertation on his own transformation from a Rome-loving celebrant of V-Day to "Dan Berrigan," a project he repeatedly (and accurately) kidded would never get me tenure.

While Dan was changing me through conversations about prayer, community, God, resistance, and poetry, I was guest to his own spiritual conversion laid out in his archived letters. On the way to publishing his correspondence with Phil in *The Berrigan Letters*, my co-editor Dan Cosacchi and I found a 1943 missive in which Dan called God a "good Soldier" and justified fighting in war. Towards the end of his life, when our relationship mostly consisted of me showing him old letters from friends and family that had been in faraway boxes for years, I handed him a copy of this one. He smiled to see how ancient it was, but when he got to this section he raised his eyebrows sharply, tilted his head back, and made a comical "O" shape with his mouth. He talked very little those latter days, but the young Dan's words spoke powerfully enough for the both of us about how dramatically he had *changed*.

And like some of those who helped mold him—Dorothy, Gandhi, Bonhoeffer, Heschel, Merton, and especially Phil—he kept transforming more radically against the impulse for safety and security that youth are told they will inevitably succumb to as they age. He was well into his forties when he first went to jail. His conversion was not glacial but certainly took what Liz [McAlister] and Phil called "time's discipline."

And despite his age, he was still ruminating on life's mysteries, not at all acting as a finished product. I recall a parade of books he plowed through between our talks, including an anvil-sized tome on Caravaggio. (It paired nicely with the impressively large bottle of spirits on his desk that seemed lower [in volume] with every visit.) He still had a growing end to be fed, still thirsted to learn. But he also acknowledged the fact of death, seemed ready for the final transformation into another kind of rebirth.

It was at his 2016 funeral that I realized how much his presence shaped me. I marched through the rain to see him off one final time with friends I never would have met if not for Dan pointing me to the Catholic Worker. He had effectively made his community mine. And afterwards, just as I was leaving the church and about to move to Charlottesville, I met the blue-haired Sue Frankel-Streit, a Catholic Worker who lived right by my soon-to-be home. We'd later go to Standing Rock together and her farm became a sacred space to me. So there was Dan, even in death, transforming my present, my future; gifting community from the coffin.

In Charlottesville I also came to know a Pentecostal reverend named Osagyefo Sekou. In the legacy of the Clergy and Laity Concerned About Vietnam that Dan cofounded, Sekou had cofounded the Clergy and Laity

Concerned About Iraq. He trained us in nonviolent confrontation before the Unite the Right Rally in 2017, where the fascist creep and white supremacist march were on full display. After one training I read an essay of his that brought Dan to mind. "When monsters say that we should lie down and die," wrote Sekou, "the art of loving and living is the sacred task of artists."

Like Sekou, Dan was an artist on the page and in the streets, but also in the soul. He was a visionary in the art of active contemplation. Even in the late stage when I came to know him, he was still painting prayer, still spilling color over onto those in fear of fading, who came knocking at the threshold of his door, his spirit. His canvas was life itself, both inner and outer, and he knew how to transmute, even transubstantiate its material. My entire relationship with him, as is true of countless others, could not be captured but maybe pointed towards with the name adopted for the 2012 Plowshares action: *Transform Now!*

I recall (somewhat rudely) asking him at ninety-two what it felt like to be done getting arrested. "Who says I'm done?" he asked, feigning indignation. He smiled playfully, but I think he meant it.

I know him only on paper as some resistance rock star changing the world. In person I knew him as this smiler in the face of one last transformation. But they both continue to work a change in me, and in reading this wonderful book I know you understand this story better than I do.

Thanks for hearing me out, Bill. And for sharing these pages with us.

Peace

Eric

Eric Martin teaches in the UCLA Center for the Study of Religion. He is part of the Catholic Worker and Charlottesville Charis communities.

— Chapter 2 —

Teacher: "Eat this Book"

> Then the voice that I had heard from heaven spoke to me again, saying, "Go, take the scroll that is open in the hand of the angel who is standing on the sea and on the land." So I went to the angel and told him to give me the little scroll; and he said to me, "Take it, and eat; it will be bitter to your stomach, but sweet as honey in your mouth."—Revelation 10:8–9

IN THE FINAL WEEKS of his underground freedom in 1970, Daniel Berrigan sat at table with William Stringfellow at his Block Island home. The board spread before a picture window overlooking New Harbor. Down the hill on the adjacent stone wall a wooden platform would be discovered suitable for placing an FBI directional microphone aimed at the window. I suppose it's possible that somewhere a record of their conversations is transcribed.

Their discussions in those days included many things: among them the book of Revelation as a political tract of nonviolent resistance. The conversation would continue as Dan studied it closely in prison and Bill wrote *An Ethic for Christians and Other Aliens in a Strange Land*. The other topic over which they brooded together was the prospect of an underground seminary after the fashion of Dietrich Bonhoeffer's Confessing Church school at Finkenwald in Germany of the 1930s. Berrigan had gone underground on the anniversary of Bonhoeffer's execution by Hitler and had begun that day a review of his biography. In it he was taken with the seminary so monastic in character. Stringfellow was similarly edified going back to the immediate post-war period and was, by the present converse, imagining a school on Block Island using the empty summer hotels to house it.

These conversations were interrupted when the infamous FBI "bird-watchers" invaded the property, coming up the drive along the adjacent wall. A storm was gathering and Dan sat in the backyard slicing apples. He rose and went out to meet his captors, leaving the fruit behind. Stringfellow, it turned out, "gathered up the remnants that nothing be lost," and consigned them to the freezer. When Berrigan returned two years later after the completion of his prison term, he reported being greeted with a spectacular banquet, including a glorious pie of (the self-same) resurrected apples rescued from Bill's freezer.[1]

It would be wrong to imagine that the move toward the seminary was itself interrupted. In point of fact, the prison time marked a kind of tryout inside the walls. From the cells of Danbury, Berrigan gathered a cohort of draft resisters, politicos, and conventional felons to learn the rule of Thich Nhat Hanh's Tien Hiep order, study Scripture, and practice resistance on the inside. He just kept teaching. As he put it:

> A classroom is where you find it. In 1970 I voyaged from Cornell, where I had taught and ministered to Danbury Prison, a slot below the Ivy League, so to speak. I felt, nonetheless, a certain rightness in the move . . . I was shortly to discover another class, in more senses than one. It was a kind of dark side of the moon; the subjects were despair, anger, violence, broken lives, racism, macho and punk, suffocation of spirit. Quite an education for the teacher . . . It was clear that some prisoners wanted desperately to flex their minds.[2]

When he emerged from Danbury in 1972, one vocational thread that lay before him was teaching. He resolved to accept only one-semester commitments, and those with the caveat that it might be interrupted by civil disobedience and its consequences. His first gig was at Woodstock College, the Jesuit school in Manhattan, just across the street from, and affiliated with, Union Seminary. It was the exception to his rule, as he stayed an entire year.

That's when I met him. A group of us Union seminarians were more than ready to welcome him. The year prior, our first, we'd been prepared by a course from Rubem Alves, the Brazilian Protestant liberation theologian then writing a book on imagination and the powers, or as he put it: resisting the "logic of the dinosaur." We'd also done a student-directed course of our own devising, on the Harrisburg Conspiracy trial.

Dan's course was on John's Apocalypse, per his conversation with Stringfellow you might say. We were reading it with the work of Jacques Ellul in the other hand. Bill would have been instrumental in conversation about

---

1. D. Berrigan, *Block Island*, 17.
2. D. Berrigan, *Ten Commandments*, 126–27.

Ellul as well, though the latter's work had also been a topic of the famous Merton retreat in 1964, particularly with respect to the technological powers. Our "class" was reading his early tract: *The Presence of the Kingdom*. By then Ellul himself had produced a commentary on the Apocalypse, then still in French, which Dan of course spoke—perhaps he had read the book. His own reading of Revelation in those days was laced with a bit of T. S. Eliot's *Four Quartets* (in the end is our beginning). He reported having memorized the *Quartets* while at Danbury. It was a discipline he undertook to survive the deadly homilies of the prison chaplain at mass. As the Father began to drone on, Dan simply applied himself to the poetic text.

In many respects Dan's lectures were nearly oracular and ecstatic utterances. We'd be scrambling to keep up in our notebooks. More than once I recall one of us saying, "Wait. What did you just say?" And he'd look up, as if coming out of a trance, to shrug and be no further help: "I dunno."

I confess I "freaked in" a bit. For a while, I could barely speak. Inner foundations had been shaken. I'd been raised in the church, yet most of what I believed, at least politically, was little more than sociology. Now the veil was torn away. I walked around dumb and silent. Berrigan noticed. The moment that he called my name down a basement hallway at Union, I consider my summons to discipleship. He invited me up to his McGiffert Hall apartment and poured a scotch, my first. That turned into weekly mornings over mint tea and talk, handing me Merton on the desert monks and Dorothy Day on the pilgrimage of poverty. Such sessions were my first experience of spiritual direction, though I'd never even heard tell of such a thing.

I know he taught Revelation courses in more than one venue in subsequent years, but I always thought that his little book *The Nightmare of God* was basically a transcription of our NYC class, post-prison. He wasn't so much teaching us to put more politics into our Scripture study as he was urging us to put more biblical savvy into our politics. His life and witness provided the authority for reading Scripture as a life-and-death matter. Prison was both geography and credential. The blood of Vietnamese children was motive. The Catonsville draft board action as liturgical poetics and the trial as theatrical drama fully filled and informed the classroom.

I remember the lectures (vividly), the readings, and the group discussions, but have nothing in my files by way of written assignments, papers. Yet he did influence work I undertook for other classes. For example, in a course on the passion of Jesus, I produced a paper detailing the suffering created by the war—it had a fifteen-page footnote which was the exegetical assignment of the class. For a course on Poetry and Theology, I analyzed Berrigan's prison poem, "Vietnamese Letter."[3] I brought his presence to the table of a Seminar on Dietrich Bonhoeffer, taught by one of Bonhoeffer's own New York friends, a colleague, theologian Paul Lehmann. And I wrote my MDiv thesis on "Resistance as Pastoral Ministry." Such like.

Instead of papers, Dan led us out of the classroom with the Bible in hand. To the Thomas Merton Center, then based at St. John the Divine, down to the Catholic Worker to meet Dorothy Day on an evening in which he spoke to clarify our thoughts. Even down to the trial of the Camden 28 (another draft board raid) where he would testify on the stand, mostly about the Sermon on the Mount. Conversations in the hall there turned into lifelong friendships. There were vigils in front of St Patrick's, walks over to Columbia to meet with students resisting Riverside Research, a university military think tank. We followed him to Danbury Prison for the release of his brother Phillip—into the waiting arms, not only of Liz McAlister and Dan, but of Abraham Heschel (who taught across the street from us and shortly crossed over to the ancestors) as well as Pete Seeger, who sang at the improvised Eucharist.

Moreover, he brought in "teaching assistants," members of the Danbury cohort, now on the street organizing. We sat with Mitch Snyder, who joined the prison group as felon (grand theft auto) and now worked with the Community for Creative Nonviolence in DC. John Bach, one of the young draft resisters, was now part of Jonah House—the community founded in Baltimore by Phillip and Liz. In those days, the MO of Jonah was to gather as a community at the house each weekend, but then some would scatter up and down the east coast to meet with smaller communities. Our little class became one of those; John would hitchhike the Jersey Turnpike to NYC each week to meet with us, study a book like Jim Douglass's *Resistance and Contemplation,* and eventually plan simultaneous actions with other groups. He was my mentor in Theological Leaflet Writing 101.

One action involved dropping an air-war banner from the Statue of Liberty. The gym floor at Riverside Church served as a banner-painting surface. But mostly I think of the liturgical actions we undertook at Riverside Research, carrying a Good Friday cross all the way from Union down to its nondescript warehouse digs on 58th Street, there to block the doors

3. See chapter 6.

and be arrested. Riverside subsequently become an ongoing witness of the Kairos Community in NY of which Dan was part.

The resistance seminary did in fact get resurrected like the apple pie. One day Berrigan brought us unexpected greetings from no less than Bill Stringfellow, including an invitation to meet and consider the idea of an underground seminary. We came to the meeting, our eager heads full of plans: location, faculty, finances? So we were utterly dumbfounded, and gradually edified, when the entire day was dedicated to Bible study, in this case 2 Thessalonians. There is a saying that goes, "To plan a party, have a party," and that applied, we were learning, to underground seminaries as well.

Dan and Bill managed to make clear that if there were to be more such gatherings, they would need to be initiated and planned by students interested. We were, and so seized the proffered initiative, organizing a series of them over the years. For the first such go-round, we secured a farm in the Berkshires and dispersed a call letter to assorted contacts, which read in part:

> The seminaries we come from tend to be parochial in their concerns, and those concerns narrow daily as financial problems make "survival" a deathly institutional preoccupation. We would gather to connect with one another, and broaden our vision of ministry. The seminaries we come from tend to follow cults of academia, worshiping professionalism and expertise. We would gather free of idolatrous enslavements. Seminarians and seminaries seem to have forgotten how to read the Bible, reducing it to an intellectual exercise, to a matter of proper critical technique. We would gather to help each other become radically biblical and biblically radical. In short, the seminaries we come from are more and more swallowed up by the culture. We would gather to come out, to turn again.[4]

Just to say, the pattern of these gatherings was simple in the extreme. A date compatible with their calendars would be set. Dan would respond often with a simple postcard with a cryptic scrawl, but clear affirmation: like "Barkus is willin'." Place would be found with sufficient sleeping space arranged (much of it on the floor or in tents). Meals were cooperative in character, anarchist as it were, with bread and a large pot of soup being mainstays.

The real feast, however, was the biblical text (Acts, say, or James or Isaiah) chosen in consultation and named in the invitation. A handful

---

4. Call letter in the author's files.

of folks, including Bill and Dan, would each take a chapter, preparing reflections with which to lead out. Then a silence would follow, with space to walk some paths or a lakeshore or even city streets. It always seemed that when we returned to the circle, the text had in the meantime read us, measured our lives, and summoned our hearts into the open. Then lo and behold, in conversation, acts of conscience could be imagined, communities formed, vocations awakened, even marriages sparked, a spirit of holy improvisation set loose.

After Woodstock/Union I know Dan went on the road to Jesuit universities to be a resident theologian or some such for a semester. I have in my letter files copies of his hilarious "final exams," poking ironies and absurdities at academia; the real exam was in how deep you took things into your life. Here's a sampling from one of the former:

> You answer all, any, or none of the following questions . . . .
>
> - Is there such a thing as a theologically indefensible position? Explain.
> - How many different ways can you spell Schillibex?
> - Has the church always taught anything? Be specific.
> - Reflect on the Seven Deadly Sins. Describe how you have integrated these in your life.
> - Does Karl Rahner believe in verbs?
> - In light of recent papal directives, discuss the hundred button cassock. Should the garment properly be unbuttoned at the top, bottom or middle? Discuss the pros and cons in light of the above, of a six-foot zipper. Given the sacred male priesthood, are not 2 zippers too much? Discuss by way of contrast, the possibilities of a hundred button fly.
> - Construct, on a single size sheet, a mockup of the Trinity.
> - If the headquarters of the western church are at Geneva and Rome, where are its hind quarters? Illustrate.
> - Taking in account the view of Norman Vincent Peale that Christ had everything going for him, and blew it, refute the Servant Songs of Isaiah.[5]

Those are from the Jesuit School at Berkeley, but he also had stints at Fordham, the University of Detroit, and others. At all of these, he left in his

---

5. On the back of an undated note from Dan, author's files.

wake new communities of resistance. The roots of Day House (the Detroit Catholic Worker) and the Detroit Peace Community can be traced directly to his visitation here.

Only add: the underground seminary rose to another round of life in Word and World: A Peoples' School.[6] It's another story, but to it and for Dan, I offer this poem:[7]

> learning the word in the shell of the world
>
> it is
> new as an egg nested high in the cleft of a rock
> teeming precariously, with life,
> and ancient, even as the rock itself
>
> fresh as manna glistening the ground
> of a wilderness camp
> convened in the company of ungulates, angels, and wild beasts.
> we travel light, learning this day
>   our daily bread—and nothing more
>
> it is living and lucid in the school of Isaiah
> harboring for decades, their mentor's edgy and sighted poems
> read, re-imagined, re-writ, performed as news
> of imperial collapse at the turn of history's hope and healing.
>
> all as we stumble, hastening to keep up
> shook by parables afoot, spun over shoulder
> by a rabbi (this image of God) schooling us in the Way by walking it
> barely sitting to teach
> till in the occupied temple court
> with spies and cops hovering
>
> practically the spot where Paul was busted
> student of Gamaliel and Stephen
> organizing a movement

6. See http://www.wordandworld.org/history.html.
7. Wylie-Kellermann, *Principalities*, vii–ix.

one road, one household, one city at a time
tell me what *ekklesia* looks like
this is what *ekklesia* looks like

and so it looked to hermits and monks of invention
trekking off again to desert huts
jumping ship from empire's smooth and bellicose arrangement
there to gather wry stories and sayings,
to ponder the sparest in a cup

what would claire or francis,
(gone begging in mendicancy) say?
taught by birds and sister moon to pray.

wending their way to Gandhi's ashram
clinging like warriors in a circle to truth
the deep thing worth dying for

Bonhoeffer had an appointment there
to re-learn the Sermon on the Mount
from a Hindu pilgrim with
salt of the earth and sea in hand.

but he was waylaid by events
necessitating a seminary underground
where he set the needle on a 78
of Negro Spirituals from Abyssinian
and translated them, guttural thick and precise,
as a stick in the spokes of a wheel—

find the cost of freedom schools buried in the ground

how does it all come round again? rise again and live?

it is in the silence broken by Audre, by Martin,
it's there in Daniel's poem telling Phil's hammer stroke,
or in Dorothy's little way

and Peter's agronomic university
the Alleluia of Bill's ashes buried

it is in the soil, the fallen grain,
the hospitable loaf passed, teeming and ancient,
hand to hand to hand

in all we have, and all we are
being enough,
it is

In his funeral homily for Dan, Steve Kelly referred to him (and Phil) as Doctors of the Church. "They retrieved for the people of God a move from preoccupation with orthodoxy to orthopraxis."[8] That's a big and formal title conferred on very few of the saints. And I wouldn't disagree. Suffice it to say: Daniel Berrigan, as for so many others, was my teacher. In a tradition, in the wholeness of his humanity, it was a gift and vocation he embraced with wit and love. Doctor? Professor? Well, something close, inseparable from poet, priest, and prophet.

8. Kelly, "Do Not Be Ruled," 20.

Pedagogical Aside: Jailhouse Teacher
(A Letter from John Bach)

November 18, 2020

Dear Bill,

Thanks for asking about Dan as teacher in prison. He taught so many of us how to be free and to enflesh the affirmation of life in the process. I marvel at the precision and power of the memories after half a century. To wit:

In what prison managers at the federal prison in Danbury, Connecticut in 1971 eventually realized was a grave mistake, they allowed Phil and Dan Berrigan to convene a weekly great books class in the education department, open to the whole prison community. Little did they know that all movements toward liberation start with people telling stories, sharing histories, and educating themselves. All real education is ultimately subversive, especially in prison, when community is built, sustained, and nourished. Dan was an integral part of that, as organizer, facilitator, educator, free (and freed) spirit, and brother.

In spite of the transient nature of the population, there was a core group of a dozen men that included not just draft resisters and draft board raiders, but bank robbers, embezzlers, car thieves, drug sellers, and breakers of other federal laws. No distinction was made by crime within the classroom or on the compound.

I was transferred to Danbury just in time for a discussion of Jonathan Swift. I'd had a scholarship to what was considered a good college, but in the first class in that prison classroom I marveled at Dan's insights, eloquence, spot-on analysis, and the implications for what passed for politics and the social contract during the American war in Vietnam. Acceptable savagery. He was by far the most engaging professor I had ever listened to, and it was, it struck me, totally free. And absolutely liberating.

Over the next four months we covered a lot of territory: two Erik Erickson psychological studies of Martin Luther, and Gandhi, the Gospel of Mark, an anthology of feminist writers, and another on Marxism. Class participants suggested books, which guaranteed a wide range of topics, part political, part spiritual, part cultural.

Dan stood in front of a blackboard, chalk in hand, breathed life into the topic with gale-force wind, and we were captivated, filled with that same life-force drive that we now understood had to be actualized.

Months later those classes eventually led to an almost miraculous clandestine printing of 300 copies of a mimeographed statement declaring a work and hunger strike by eleven inmates. The issues ranged from the continuing war in Vietnam (and stating solidarity with the prisoners in the infamous tiger cages), to the racist and unjust system of granting or refusing paroles, and also specifically demanding Dan's release because of his fragile health.

It is rather astounding that in a culture where limited self-interest governs every aspect of a constricted life, inmates would risk and certainly be punished with transfers, and additional time on their sentences, increased separation from their homes and families, on behalf of another inmate. And see that as part of being liberated in captivity. Such was the devotion that Dan inspired.

That teaching and sharing went on in every aspect of prison life, and Dan was at the center of much of it. Iron bars melted and concrete walls crumpled. The oasis began crowding out the desert. Miracle of miracles: freedom was no longer determined solely by what side of the wall you were on. The chow hall had four-person tables, and we joked about having sign-up sheets, such was the demand for being in his presence.

In the evening we would congregate on the yard's bleachers watching some magnificent sunsets. Dan would brew concoctions of coffee, hot chocolate, with melted Snickers bars that were shared amid all the laughter. It was he who labeled the buzzer summoning us for the 9:00 count as the "elephant fart." And said of an especially uptight hack that you could put a brand new pencil up his butt and after one walking revolution around the yard it would emerge fully sharpened. We parted company with the common refrain, "Stay Strong."

There appeared an underground newspaper (*The Shit-House Press*) that managed to stay underground and widely circulated for a couple of editions. The editors put out a couple of pages of copy in longhand, and stapled a few blank pages for additional news and comments, solicited from the readership; truly a free press. There were no bylines, for obvious reasons, but here's one that appeared in Dan's unmistakable artistic scrawl:

> Hardly one Correctional [sic] Officer has his life together, yet
> they are hired to help us get our lives together. What a laugh. Like

monkeys on ladders, the higher they climb the more their asses show. But how many of us have our lives together? How many beyond the crooks' scam? Beyond the hustle? Beyond mistreating our women? Moral: monkeys change when men change first.

A year later after both Dan and Phil had left Danbury, and amid all the increased tension after the prison uprising at Attica, there occurred a nine-day, unequivocally nonviolent work stoppage. The roots could be traced in part to that great books class and the lessons learned about enfleshing the glorious principles we had read and discussed and made immediate in our lives. It was the realization of the Beloved Community and Dan lived on among us, as teacher, prophet, and brother. He taught us how to be free.

Thanks again, Bill. Please convey a tip o' the hat to Denise and the *Geez* community.

John

Sentenced under the Youth Act and so serving three years in federal prison for draft resistance, John Bach is a former inmate with Daniel Berrigan, a cofounder of Jonah House and The Whale's Tale, a house painter for a living, and Quaker chaplain at Harvard University.

—— Chapter 3 ——

Brother: To Phil, on Reading
Their Correspondence

THIS BOOK,[1] *THE BERRIGAN Letters*,[2] arrived here by post unbidden from Orbis, just days before the news of Daniel's death on April 30, 2016. I carried it east to the wake and funeral. It was soaked with rain in my pack during the procession from Maryhouse to St Francis Xavier. Its stiff warp and wrinkle is a sweet remembrance.

This publication edited by two of his friends, Daniel Cosacchi and Eric Martin, was initiated by Dan himself with such events on the horizon. It is a gift, even if one that shows signs of the haste of getting it into his frail and failing hands. Even counting Berrigan-Merton and Berrigan-Dorothy Day, there may be no relationship more significant to the rise of North American Christian conscience against warmaking than the fraternal love these letters trace. That the two, in collars, shared the cover of *Time* magazine during the war in Indochina is small measure. Liz McAlister, Phil's wife and partner in resistance community, contributes a preface that is the best possible account of that brotherhood, loving and precise. One might hope some day to see Phil and Liz's correspondence, well edited, much of which would be from prison and some of which is already made notorious by the FBI.

Phil was the younger, though one might easily miss that guess—hardly the little brother. It was really he who pulled and cajoled Dan into the Catonsville Nine draft board raid (1968) as into the first Plowshares action at General Electric's nuclear weapons plant in King of Prussia, Pennsylvania (1980). As he wrote after the former: "[Tom] Lewis and I can't say enough about what

1. Wylie-Kellermann, Review of *The Berrigan Letters*, 4.
2. Cosacchi and Martin, eds., *Letters*.

it meant to have you with us. Certainly the fiery seven if not nine, looked to you for marvelous insights, good grace, and humor . . . You've meant the Church to me, at its best and noblest. And no one else has that asset and privilege, to the extent that I have. Luv ya." (May 25, 1968.)[3]

The letters begin with Dan's earnest youthful piety in formation by the Jesuits, set beside Phil's joining up with the Air Corps to fight in the Good War, and so precede both their conversions to nonviolence. Dan early wrote a blessing: "To realize that the soldiering of this war is a vocation too—that would solve some of your difficulties and loneliness and the vague worries too shadowy for definition, wouldn't it, Phil? . . . And your part is to play the game (as you are doing superbly) looking to Him Who was a good Soldier—unto death." (Sept. 15, 1943.)[4] At war's end, Philip hitchhiked to Woodstock to celebrate with song, drink, and a flag-borne victory procession around the seminary.

Two decades later, Phil is pioneering a new form of nonviolent (even liturgical) direct action in the destruction of draft files. As he explains to his brother, "Sorry I didn't make the action clearer—it must have caused you great concern. No, I would never do anything that would harm people physically—but the property that is part of these bloody gearboxes, thass another thing." (October 1967.)[5]

Their conversions were gradual, nurtured by racial struggle and travels—to Europe and the Global South—all reflected. But other sources would be needed to fully map that story. The glimpses are striking but must be sought in the fits and starts of archival availability.

In some periods the letters are only in one of their voices; some periods (like 1943–51 or 1955–62) are pure silence. The care of saving or the changing of archivists figure in.

Dan mentions visiting Dorothy Day in the forties, but she doesn't come up in this correspondence until 1964. There is reference to Merton, but nothing about the famous Gethsemani peacemakers retreat in the fall of that same year. (Best to read this with Gordon Oyer's recent account, *Pursuing The Spiritual Roots of Protest*, in hand.) Martin Luther King's "Letter From a Birmingham Jail" is highly lauded, but his "Beyond Vietnam" speech at Riverside Church, equally a watershed, or his assassination the following year find no mention—even though riots following the

---

3 Cosacchi and Martin, eds., *Letters,* 40–41.

4. Cosacchi and Martin, eds., *Letters,* 7.

5. Cosacchi and Martin, eds., *Letters,* 37.

latter fully interrupted Phil's trial for the Baltimore Four action for three days.[6] I looked immediately for Dan's time teaching at the University of Detroit in the early 1970s. Though it was a slightly harrowing experience for him, living above drug dealers in the downstairs flat, that was a time that seeded Day House and the Worker community here in Detroit. Alas, it falls in a one-sided stretch where Daniel's voice is absent. Likewise, for the years of the Underground Seminary that he helped shape with William Stringfellow, first in Massachusetts, then in Michigan. It would be lovely to see his comments to Phil.

These letters were not written with an eye toward publication. Most have a newsy, casual, pointed, and trusting intimacy. Phil, in particular, can occasionally drop a blunt aside about a friend, even a dear one, that in publication could sting with frankness. And Daniel can level the order or the academics with a deft swipe. This on teaching in Berkeley:

> Today sixty for the Revelation 'seminar,' same sequence, I blatt for an hour, then groups. We'll see. There is much disaffection on holy hill, the Jebs plus others are now faced with an outpouring of folks and different footwork; their style is the immemorial bonhomie pipe puffing inconsequential banalities of the 60s, 50s, 40s, 30s, etc. I think they'll just drag out the armadillo sleeping bags & crawl in. But maybe not. (January 1980.)[7]

The 1980s are a period in which the two are archivally on the same page so the conversation is a lively back and forth. The energy of 1980, movement-wise, is amazing. Jonah House was organizing weekly actions at the Pentagon (in which the Detroit Peace Community, thereby named, participated). Dan, working the West Coast, is steering students to the street and east. Though the brothers are necessarily circumspect and silent about the first Plowshares as it approaches, it bursts into that scene taking direct action to yet another level and jump-starting a movement still ongoing. In its aftermath the letters show them playing inside/outside, with Phil and the seven being in, as in jail, and Dan working the outside, navigating and interpreting. Dan once wrote to me: "Phil peddles hardware, I peddly software." A telling snip.

Their roles, their voices differ, like their handwriting. Phil's steady, neat, forward-leaning, clear. Dan's a poetic and less predictable scrawl

---

6. John Dear identifies King's assassination as a moving impetus for the Catonsville action. Dear, ed., *Essential*, 25.

7. Cosacchi and Martin, eds., *Letters*, 168.

with color, illustrations, and marginal markings. The collection includes no glimpse of either brother's hand. I'm remembering that once, in a book from the underground days post-Catonsville, Dan himself published most of a letter from prison handwritten on the inside cover of *America is Hard to Find*.

Philip's daughter, Frida, endorsed *The Berrigan Letters* with a caution: "Watch out! This book is going to make you pick up a pen, paper and envelope, and visit the venerable old Post Office . . . After reading these epistles, you will be compelled to write the people you care about and make indelible your affection and appreciation. You have been warned."

It's not beside the point to note the downward spiral from email to Facebook to Twitter, which so cheapens and corrupts our correspondence. We are technically seduced. Letter-writing as resistance? This book tells a relationship, a history, a style of faith and conscience in the world. But it also tells and urges a discipline of time, a discipline of relationship and community, a handmade discipline of love.

Freedom Struggle Aside: A Brotherly
Conversion Narrative

Dan may have nudged Philip to priesthood, but Phil decisively pulled Dan into Catonsville and Plowshares—and long before that toward the Freedom Struggle, with all its conversional possibility and import, as Eric Martin has fully demonstrated.[8]

Phil had been disgusted by the racism he witnessed during Army basic training in the South. When he answered the call to priesthood, encouraged by Dan, he chose the order of St. Joseph because of their commitment to the African American community, but he shortly became critical of the structural segregation so readily accepted by the order. He saw it up close in his assignment to a New Orleans church. As Martin writes, "The Josephites interpreted his critique of their approach as malicious when he suggested they spent too much time trying to save souls and ignoring the spiritual links to the concrete present in which Black people were dying."[9] By 1957 he held memberships in the Fellowship of Reconciliation, the NAACP, Southern Christian Leadership Conference (SCLC), the Urban League, and the Student Nonviolent Coordinating Committee (SNCC).

Dan was then teaching at Le Moyne College in Syracuse. At Phil's behest they set up something of a tag-team swap, with Dan sending white students to New Orleans for summer work in the Josephite mission center of a Black neighborhood, and Phil sending young Black students north for college scholarships and continued learning under Dan—something they termed an "interracial apostolate."[10]

Then, in 1961, came the "Freedom Rides" organized by the Congress of Racial Equality (CORE), with interracial groups traveling into the South toward New Orleans by bus, publicly testing segregation laws en route. This caught the brothers' attention. The first two interstate actions were met by mobs, burning one of the buses, and bloodily beating the passengers (including one known personally by me).

As Dan wrote to a young Catholic Worker, Karl Meyer, who was his pastoral and spiritual advisee:

8. For my understanding of this history and the broad strokes outline for part of this section, even for materials that are the Berrigan bones set here, I am indebted to Eric Martin's dissertation chapter, "I Came on Another Way: The Civil Rights Movement, 1957–1963." Martin, "Conversion."

9. Martin, "Conversion," 148.

10. Martin, "Conversion," 151.

We are of course experiencing the birth pangs of the southern crisis, more and more precipitated by the "midwife" tactics of the freedom riders . . . As usual, the Catholic response is negligible; we will pay for this before Christ, if God is God . . . All this would cause any son of the Church to weep for the Church and to suffer inwardly for her who is, in us untrue to the Christ who is also within us. I take it as one of the greatest gifts of my priesthood that through yourself and my brother the priest, I am allowed some small part in those issues . . . The whole earth is in childbirth, and the new man does not wish to be born, because birth into adulthood, where we can accept God and one another, is a bloody business.[11]

Together, in August of 1961, the brothers determined to make identical requests to their superiors for permission to join one of the Freedom Rides. The buses were finding no shortage of Protestant pastors to fill the seats, but they, in effect, proposed to be the first Catholic priests to be arrested in the movement.

Daniel was denied it and he stood down. He had come to readiness for the direct action of civil disobedience, but not for ecclesial disobedience. Phil, in turn, along with a second Josephite, was granted permission, and flew to CORE headquarters in New York to meet with James Farmer and work out arrangements for entering the ride in Jackson, Mississippi. While there, they also laid the groundwork for its reporting in Catholic media. Their plans, however, were scuttled when word got out too quickly of the momentous priestly involvement. They were mobbed by journalists as they prepared to board a plane. News reached the bishop in Jackson, who threatened the order if they were not called back. They were, and honored the directive, though for both Phil and Dan this experience of Church authority would rankle their conscience going forward.[12]

About this time, stemming from an article in *The Catholic Worker*, Daniel resumed a correspondence and now friendship with Thomas Merton. The year following, 1962, he visited the monastery, Gethsemani Abbey in Kentucky, and addressed the novices. A letter to Merton suggests a smoldering annoyance with church officialdom.

News from all over; after prodding by the Cath. Interracial Council, the bishop here wrote all the priests of the diocese, urging them to cease resisting efforts of the relocation office, in placing negroes

11. D. Berrigan to Karl Meyer (June 17, 1961), in Martin, "Conversion," 153.
12. Martin, "Conversion," 154–57.

in white neighborhoods. But the letter contained this gem (which is really worth another piece of paper) "As Bishops and priests, our first duty in this matter is to preserve our property values and neighborhoods, and to teach these people the same values for which we stand." *Proh dolor* [Alas] . . . It was in effect, a massive episcopal blessing of selfishness as though a chi-rho truck, water tank and all, had passed through the sacred outer neighborhoods, to sprinkle homes, families, lawns, all, with the blessing of God.[13]

Meanwhile, at Le Moyne, having denied Daniel permission to start an off-campus community, the college reversed itself only to suffer certain regret. The backstory was that Berrigan had quietly encouraged his "spiritual advisee" Karl Meyer to move to Syracuse and start a Catholic Worker house in a low-income neighborhood. Another tag-team educational venture closer to home was clearly envisioned. The diocesan bishop got wind of it, as well as Daniel's connection, and peremptorily shut the project down. Now granted permission (previously denied) to start International House, a living community preparing students for transnational service, he located a building in a poor neighborhood adjacent and moved in with a dozen students. Their first task was to make the place liveable, including the basement chapel, simply and beautifully appointed. As foundation for work they would undertake in Mexico, the group began researching the absentee slumlords who ruled their neighbors. As he urged them, "Who was accountable, say, for an uninhabitable derelict building, a crowded slum block? Who collected rent and refused to make repairs?" As it turned out, the Who included a number of college benefactors. Publication of the list was problematic to administrators, and in a taste of future exile, Dan's sabbatical to Paris, Eastern Europe, and South Africa was hastened apace.[14]

Berrigan wrote to Merton capturing the extent of his frustration and the seriousness of his considerations.

> I have the sinking feeling sometimes of chucking it all over, the pseudo obedience cult that protects all the fences, and going to Birmingham—my temptation wd. be a great deal stronger if 1) I felt I could ever again be able to work as a priest 2) I knew of some institution or Bishop anywhere who wd. protect a man who had gone in for civil disobedience + church disobedience but who still wants to be a Catholic and a priest. Is this wild talk? . . . What is needed + what should be possible is a small group of men who

13. D. Berrigan to Merton (May 16, 1962), Martin, "Conversion," 159.

14. Forest, *Lion's Den*, 48–49, 51–53.

were living in the exposed way of the Fraternities but who would be free to break up their sacred housekeeping in the name of justice and social need—going to jail, freedom rides, etc., at call, and then wd. resume things afterward when the need was past, if such was God's will for them . . . Shd. not a real contemplative life issue in + be allowed a freedom such as this? Or what is it for?[15]

Though in response Merton confessed to harboring such thoughts himself ("the same idea has come to me many times"), he urged temperance from anything drastic lest the spiritual momentum of God's work in his life be ruined. When Phil glimpsed the letter, he wrote back, "Merton's letter was marvelous—I guess he knows your dilemma and mine because it's also his own. It did a great deal to quiet some of the unanswered questions," adding, "In what context can you and I do most good? I am of the opinion now that it is within the Church."[16]

In that context, even with their patience wearing thin, the brothers joined in once again asking permission to participate in public political action, this time the 1963 March on Washington for Jobs and Freedom. Phil, now transferred to the Bronx and, working in Harlem, was already attending organizing meetings with A. Philip Randolph, director of the event, and had begun coordinating joint efforts with Protestants and Catholics.[17]

Together at the march they record an "immense profound spiritual force" enveloping the crowd. Even sleep-deprived from travel by bus and train, they delighted to sit side by side in the sun listening to the speeches. This is to say, they certainly heard the sermonic crescendos of Martin King's speech—along with the voices of Marian Anderson, Mahalia Jackson, James Farmer, and John Lewis.

Upon return they published, over both their names, a report and appeal in a Syracuse paper, *The Post-Standard*:

> We believe that if the truth is told (and it has not often been told by white men), Aug. 28 was much more truly the hour for the white man than for the black . . . We were learning again what it meant to be Americans. We were learning it firsthand from those who were willing to suffer and weep and die in order to be Americans. We were learning much that we had forgotten or neglected or actively despised in our own heritage. We were learning, as one of their

15. D. Berrigan to Merton (June 14, 1963), unpublished. Martin, "Conversion," 161.

16. Phil to Daniel (July 1963), Cosacchi and Martin, eds., *Letters*, 19–20.

17. See Martin, "Conversion," 164.

speakers said, that until all Americans are free, no American is free . . . We ask them to continue their picketing, their sit-ins, all the forms of peaceful protest which they can devise . . . And we earnestly ask that white Syracusans will support and join in these efforts—efforts which are both a civic and a sacred service.[18]

The word *sacred* in that last phrase, as Eric Martin puts it, is "a nod toward what would become [Berrigan's] expansive view of where the Word of God might be found. The question the brothers pose to the readers was likely taken most seriously by themselves: 'In the face of this massive purpose and dignity, can we return with quiet consciences to unchanged lives?' For the brothers, the answer would clearly be no."[19]

Almost immediately afterward, Daniel flew off to Paris and parts east or south for his famous sabbatical. What bears mention here is the visit to South Africa. Invited by The Grail, a lay women's organization doing feminist, interracial, ecumenical, and eventually creation-based theology and liturgy, he gave a number of talks to their organization, but also took opportunity to speak with Catholic clergy and bishops particularly in relation to the anti-apartheid struggle.[20]

In one of those, he camped out on Camus's phrase that the townspeople in his novel had suffered the plague because they forgot to be modest.

> I found the words disturbingly on the mark. The immodesty of the racist regime of South Africa was apparent. But the plague could by no means be isolated there, as a matter of either principle or fact. Who could dwell in America and be ignorant of a like pretension, pride of place, intransigent racism infecting us also?[21]

I had heard tell of this invite. A member of my church in Detroit, Shirley Beaupre (now of blessed memory), notorious for neighborhood work in our community and long-sta/nding participant in The Grail, had worked with them in South Africa. She approached me after a sermon to say, "You know, we hosted Dan Berrigan there," and then told a story I no longer, to my dismay, remember.

His most remarkable experiences were met in the townships. When I was in seminary I read and passionately marked up Dan's account in

18. Martin, "Conversion," 165–66.

19. Martin, "Conversion," 167.

20. Martin, "Conversion," 206–16.

21. D. Berrigan, *Dwell,* 160–61.

"Journey from Sharpeville to Selma," of preaching in Johannesburg on Good Friday, 1964.[22] However, it took John Dear, Dan's friend and literary executor, to send me back to those urgent markings.[23]

> The Gospel of Saint John was read in Zulu. And they crucified Him there; it was about the third hour . . . The sea of color, the immobile intent faces, men, women, children, hundreds strong, seated on the earthen floor. What could a white man say to them? What could a white priest say? He could say something surely; he might even say a new thing. He might say that Christ had died for all men, even for white men. He could take up his cross, hammered together by fate, propped up, waiting, visible to all. In South Africa, his cross was simply the fact of being a white man with some remnant of conscience. He could say in public, while the Special Branch Police lounged against the walls taking notes, that he was unworthy of his black brothers; that some day, the white man might conceivably leave off being their executioner.[24]

He confessed that the Gospel in Zulu fell strange upon his ears: "sibilants and the clicking of tongues, with only the names Jesus, Mary, Peter, John coming through." He could barely remember what he hoped to say.

> But at the end, the veneration of the Cross. A great wave starts forward: mothers with children, young men, the very old. Three priests move among them, holding the crucifix to their lips. And spontaneously, as is the way with Africans, the chant starts; first, as one voice, hardly rising above the sough of bare feet, that sound which above all sounds is like the sea, on a mild evening. The song is the Zulu dirge for a fallen warrior. They are bearing Him homeward to his village after battle. His name is Jesus, great King, black Warrior. Easily, with infinite delicacy and naturalness, the song breaks into harmony; two parts, then four, then eight, as a yolk divides, or a cell . . . Jesus, great Warrior, we mourn you. O the beauty, the youth, the empty place. Who shall plead for us, who shall lift our faces, who shall speak wisdom?
>
> The Zulus have a saying: he who is behind must run faster than he who is in front. Even to the Cross. Even when the Cross is held in white hands. Shall the white man time us, even to the Cross? Does he any longer even know the way?[25]

22. D. Berrigan, "Journey from Sharpeville to Selma," *Consequences*, 63–73.

23. See Dear, ed., *Essential*, 54–60.

24. D. Berrigan, *Consequences*, 68–69.

25. D. Berrigan, *Consequences*, 70.

Upon return Dan spent time solidifying the Catholic Peace Fellowship hatched in Europe on his sabbatical, but almost immediately thereafter facing preparations for the famous November retreat at Merton's place. Gordon Oyer details an account of the company, context, and content of the gathering in *Pursuing the Spiritual Roots of Protest.*[26] He describes the events leading up to the retreat. The American war in Southeast Asia was escalating and the month prior China had detonated its own atomic bomb to join the nuclear club. A year before, following the March on Washington, four Black children, Addie Mae Collins, Cynthia Wesley, Carole Robertson, and Denise McNair, were killed in the bombing of Birmingham's 16th Street Baptist Church—and in just months preceding the retreat, the bodies of SNCC workers James Cheney, Andrew Goodman, and Michael Schwerner had been pulled from a Mississippi swamp. Merton wrote to Berrigan feeling "sick up to the teeth . . . [with] explanations about where we are going because where we are going is . . . over the falls. We are in a new river and we don't know it."[27]

Oyer recounts the jockeying and crisscrossing of invitations, the most striking of which is that Martin Luther King, Jr. and Bayard Rustin (King's nonviolent guide in Montgomery and lead organizer of the Washington March) were among the invitees and "wanted to come." Up to the last minute, Merton was still expecting Rustin, but it turned out he joined Martin, who had cancelled for a trip to Oslo, Norway to receive the Nobel Prize for Peace.[28]

The Peace Prize was urgent, to be sure, and altered Martin Luther King's vocation. Not in the sense of inflation, but of a certain broadening. In his speech "A Time to Break Silence: Beyond Vietnam," he named it as a global vocation. Indeed, it was among the answers to those who

> ask the question, "Aren't you a civil rights leader?" and thereby mean to exclude me from the movement for peace, I have this further answer . . . another burden of responsibility was placed upon me in 1964; and I cannot forget that the Nobel Peace Prize was also a commission, a commission to work harder than I had ever worked before for "the brotherhood of man." This is a calling that takes me beyond national allegiances . . .[29]

26. Oyer, *Spiritual Roots.*

27. Oyer, *Spiritual Roots,* 22.

28. Oyer, *Spiritual Roots,* 43, 46, 49.

29. King, "Break Silence," *Testament,* 233–34.

However, the absence of King and Rustin at the retreat is of enormous moment. The Catholic left anti-war movement, and especially the roots of Catonsville and the draft board actions, can be spiritually traced directly to that retreat. Yet, it had been conceived by Merton and friends more broadly. In the "Breaking Silence" speech against the war, at Riverside Church, King was attempting to link more fully the anti-war movement and the Freedom Struggle. What if that fusion had been forged earlier in the movement friendships, seeded and grown in the prayer and reflection of Gethsemani?

Rustin and King would certainly have brought different answers to Merton's lead question of "By what right do we protest?" Their response would have been more ontological—grounded in their very being of Blackness in America. And Martin had articulated the source and shape of that right from the cell of a Birmingham jail.[30]

The retreat, powerful and spiritually resonant as it was, ended up being all white men. That can only be counted a great loss. One is left to imagine what might otherwise have been. Merton wrote to Dan proposing a subsequent retreat to include women like Dorothy Day, Joan Baez, and Rosemary Radford Reuther. And in mid-April of 1968, he planned one that would host King, Vincent Harding, and Thich Naht Hanh[31]—but King was assassinated on April 4, and Merton himself would be dead by the end of the year. Imagination all but silenced.

In March of 1965, Dan and Phil answered King's call to come to Selma in the wake of Bloody Sunday the week prior. He wrote an account for *Commonweal* that begins with a litany of death, after the fashion of a Black Lives Matter street presence, naming names, calling out the cops, and recounting stories:

> It was in the air of Selma; the air bore it like a groan—the memories of some twenty years. Through these town roads, the body of a black man, roped like a venison to the sheriff's car, had been driven into the Negro area. Go slow—slow. Let them see who's in charge here. It was in the air. Fifteen years ago a black man, arrested "for talkin' back" on the word of a cranky white woman, had been murdered in Selma jail. "An unknown policeman" had entered his cell and shot him. His body was dumped off on his family. No verdict, no investigation. But the town has not forgotten.
>
> It is still in the air. Jimmy Lee Jackson, shot in Marion for defending his mother against a trooper's club, died in Good Samaritan

30. King, "Birmingham Jail," *Testament*, 289–302.
31. Oyer, *Spiritual Roots*, 234.

Hospital here. He had powder burns on the skin of his belly. The barrel had been pushed to its closest range, and fired twice. The Negroes remembered that night. When they tried to send hearses from Selma to Marion to pick up the wounded, lying untended in the streets, their answer had come from the sheriff's office; come in here, you'll get what the rest got; I'll dump you in the river.[32]

His account of the days, which I quote here at length, likewise named the "nonviolent war" that had been declared.

The false peace is interdicted. The Negroes have seen to that; from Martin Luther King to the farm hand who shows up to march on Tuesday with Monday's bandage still bloody on his head. Indeed, the trooper is right when he cries, zooming like a tortured gadfly on his motorcycle from end to end of the marchers: "I've never seen anything like this in all my ——— life!"

Neither has the nation. Neither has the Church. Who ever heard of a Church, North or South, that has rung, day after day, week after week, with the unending songs, the prayers, the sermons; a Church that spilled into the streets a people ready for whatever hell the troopers are ready to bring down on them: dogs, horses, whips, tear gas, billies? What liturgy prepares men and women and children for Lingo and Clark and Connor? What faith arms men by forbidding them arms, tells them to march when they can, to kneel when they cannot, to face the oppressor—maybe even to convert him? The questions are fierce, and for the moment (for White Americans) unanswerable. But the point is clear; the questions are real questions, as real as the broken bones and the blood; as real as the new hope . . .

[T]he newsmen were not sure why we were there. They were not even convinced that we knew why; one of them asked us, in words that were not especially flattering: why have the Catholics gotten into the act? We were not sure either, in a way that could easily be formulated. But it was something like an ethic of the guts; some things cannot be disposed of, in peace, by moral tics over headlines, even in 1965 . . .

It was worse, and better, than one had imagined. It may have been all the clerics, the white faces among the black. But there was no charge of the helmeted ring; they stood there, they didn't give an inch; but they didn't move in either. And in Selma, after the past week, that was something new.

---

32. Reprinted in Berrigan, *Consequences,* 65–66. See also Dear, ed., *Essential,* 55–58.

In front, the white priest, the rabbi and the Negro minister confronted Clark. The newsmen moved close, the TV took it all in; five minutes of passionate exchange, then the decision. A cleric in front turned to the line, spoke quietly, and knelt. Men and women and children went down on knee, as though under the pressure of some sudden wind. The TV commentator said it into his mike, stepping among the crouching figures to get his pictures. But we already knew it: "It looks like another long night in Selma."[33]

Denied permission to write a book together, the brothers wrote separate ones. Dan's included the excerpts above in an essay, and Phil's was *No More Strangers*, which Kwame Ture, still then Stokely Carmichael, endorsed for the cover saying Phil was "the only white man who knows where it's at."

In the fall of 1965, Daniel was a cofounder of Clergy and Laity Concerned (CALC). He claimed the idea came from Rabbi Abraham Heschel—to organize a religious response to the war. He noted, "The announcement, among the Jesuits, was badly received. And with other events gathering their lightning, our resolve would be part of the high drama of my departure."[34]

They convened a gathering in New York City of some 100 people to establish the organization. Martin Luther King, Jr. was among the handful of Black clergy who attended. In what would become perhaps the organization's most notorious event, in April of 1967 they hosted Dr. King's "Breaking the Silence—Beyond Vietnam" speech at Riverside Church. Drafted with assistance from Vincent Harding, King delivered the classic address with Heschel seated in the chancel behind him. (Berrigan was not present, then teaching on the West Coast.) It named the "giant triplets" of "racism, militarism, and extreme materialism" that could only be defeated with a "revolution of values."

For the first celebration of the Martin Luther King, Jr. national holiday, January 20, 1986, Dan was invited to speak at Columbia University (just up the street from where he lived, an institution sprawling large in his own neighborhood). He connected King's death with the truth of the giant triplets. "After King's speech at Riverside Church denouncing the Vietnam War, Johnson withdrew all federal protection, and shortly thereafter, Dr. King was murdered."[35] But he held out King's life and witness as a measure of the university itself.

---

33. Reprinted in D. Berrigan, *Consequences*, 66, 68, 75.

34. D. Berrigan, *Dwell*, 179.

35. D. Berrigan, "Martin Luther King, Jr. and the Arm of Justice," in *Testimony*, 98.

What would Columbia look like if Dr. King's dream were embodied here? The question is a serious one. If it were idly put, or not posed at all, as is usual on such occasions, we had best spare our breath and go on with the business of Columbia, which is hand in glove with the business of America . . .

It is too easy, too foreign to the austere style of Dr. King, to let ourselves off, in favor of excoriating Big Business or Big Military, or for that matter Big Learnery. The appetite and ambitions that fuel all of these burn away in ourselves. The rip-off of real-estate, the control of rent and rates, the mauling and eviction of tenants, the vast portfolios, the millions flowing from grateful tycoons who were taught their game here, the CIA present on campus, both recruiting and indoctrinating—these speak not only of the vocational appetite of Columbia, they speak of ourselves.[36]

He concluded reciting the crucial excerpt from the King's speech at Riverside Church, just three blocks away.

I am convinced that if we are to get on the right side of the world revolution, we as a nation must undergo a radical revolution of values. We must rapidly begin the shift from a thing-oriented society to a person-oriented society. When machines and computers, profit motives and property rights, are considered more important than people, the giant triplets of racism, extreme materialism, and militarism are incapable of being conquered . . . A nation that continues year after year to spend more money on military defense than on programs of social uplift is approaching spiritual death. America, the richest and most powerful nation in the world, can well lead the way in this revolution of values. There is nothing except a tragic death wish to prevent us from molding a recalcitrant reordering of our priorities so that the pursuit of peace will take precedence over the pursuit of war. There is nothing to keep us from molding a recalcitrant status quo with bruised hands until we have fashioned it into a brotherhood and sisterhood. We still have a choice today: nonviolent coexistence or violent co-annihilation.[37]

A year later, on the second MLK national holiday, Dan confronted the triplets, and was arrested for it, at Riverside Research, a Columbia think tank moved off-campus in hopes of quiet dissociation. Military work of many varieties, including submarine tracking and Star Wars planning,

36. D. Berrigan, *Testimony,* 95.

37. As quoted in D. Berrigan, *Testimony,* 100–101.

takes place there. With friends from the Harlem-based Emmaus House, he vigiled, poured blood, sang, and prayed.[38]

My own commitment to work with the Poor People's Campaign: A National Movement for Moral Revival, is rooted in their organizing around the triplets and picking up the work King was undertaking when he was struck down by state assassination.[39] The triplets are sometimes identified as issues, or cultural pathologies, or simply ideologies. I count them as the reigning principalities in US empire. It's also important to note (as the Campaign, in fact, does) that in response to each of these there arose a movement of resistance and transformation. Hence, the freedom struggle, the anti-war movement, and the economic justice movement (labor unions, welfare rights organizations, housing and homeless unions, and the like). At the Riverside Church "Breaking the Silence" CALC speech, King was seeking to align anti-war and freedom struggles. During the year following, he was building the original Poor Peoples' Campaign, which sought to draw both together with economic justice struggles. That, in my view, was the enormous threat he posed and the reason for his assassination. Indeed, he was killed supporting the sanitation workers (AFSME) strike in Memphis.

I give thanks for the Kings Bay Plowshares—Elizabeth McAlister, Martha Hennessy, Steve Kelly (SJ), Patrick O'Neill, Mark Colville, Carmen Trotta, and especially Clare Grady who consistently stressed in discernment that their action of blood and hammers at the Georgia Trident submarine base should expressly name the triplets. They acted on April 4, 2018—the fiftieth anniversary of Martin King's assassination and also the anniversary of his "Breaking the Silence" speech. They were convicted and have all endured prison sentences.

Dan spoke of the spiritual resources required for such actions and their consequences:

> King declared, "the church is the place you go out from." He started in the church and went from there, breaking down segregation, economic injustice, and denouncing the Vietnam War . . . [B]eing equally fearful of living and dying, we have yet to experience resurrection, which I translate, "the hope that hopes on."
>
> A blasphemy against this hope is named deterrence, or Trident submarines, or star wars, or preemptive strike, or simply, any

38. Berrigan, *Dwell*, 342–43.

39. https://www.poorpeoplescampaign.org/.

nuclear weapon . . . That is why we speak again and again of 1980 and all the Plowshares actions since, how some continue to labor to break the demonic clutch on our souls of the ethic of Mars, of wars and rumors of wars, inevitable wars, just wars, necessary wars, victorious wars, and say our no in acts of hope. For us, all of these repeated arrests, the interminable jailings, the life of our small communities, the discipline of nonviolence, these have embodied an ethic of resurrection.[40]

Just so, indeed.

---

40. D. Berrigan, "An Ethic of Resurrection," *Testimony*, 220–25.

— Chapter 4 —

Priest: A Sacramental Ethic

Said; a cleric worth his salt
will salt his bread with tears, sometimes.
will break bread
which is the world's flesh, with the world's poor,
count this his privilege and more—

And called Saint Paul for exemplar
whose fingers stitched the church a robe,
its crude device
a Christ crucified, wrought of his workman hands
which foul dust had sealed
utter and unforeseen, priest and lord.

No disdain must stain the workman's hands
that such task own
It is all one, I cried. The Lord
upbears the poor man's hand in His, His fruit.
Gospel has it so; one, grape, tendril, shoot and root.

The confession of humanity is our honor, clerics.
Celibate, father—that irony
time urges to term—
You are the poor man's food.
Or great Burgundy, rotting, sours time's ground.[1]

1. D. Berrigan, "Homily," *Risen Bread*, 3–4.

Finally, in June of 1952, amid considerable wonderment and rejoicing, I was ordained. The event was accounted at the time as a grace, and still is. Numerous photos were taken on that day of days, whose high drama time both caught and caught up with and eventually rendered both quaint and inviolate. For all that was to follow, and threaten and undermine, the anointing of ordination was a momentous healing and enlightenment. It justified the long haul and its sweat and tears, it struck a light that has never been extinguished. The healer and lighter of lamps was the then Archbishop of Boston, Richard Cushing. He performed the ordination at a tornado pace and pitch. Each of us was caught up. When his great bassoon sounded, announcing this or that stage of the proceeding, one could entertain no least doubt that the gift offered was indeed being conferred. The chariot swung low, and swept one up. And I had at last become what I was called to be . . . I was a priest at last. It was Year One of my life or the first day of a new creation. I knew not which, nor cared greatly. I went out into the sunshine, blinking with the wonder of it all, to greet and bless my family.—Daniel Berrigan, *To Dwell in Peace*[2]

FOR HIS FUNERAL IN New York's St. Francis Xavier Church on W. 16th Street, Dan was dressed, in his coffin, in full priestly regalia. It struck me as an irony, to say the least. One had to wonder how long it was since he had vested so.

It's hardly the same, but it did call to mind Dan's friend, Ken Feit, former Jesuit turned mendicant fool. Stringfellow and Towne underwrote Feit's tuition to the Barnum and Bailey clown school in Florida and he once workshopped a bunch of us in discerning our clown walks, voices, and faces. He had an amazing patchwork coat with pieces of fabric from all the places in the world he had visited, learned from, and performed his foolery. A vestment truly. Each patch had a story or several beneath it, or a nonsense poem, which he could tell at the drop of a hat should you point to one. When he died in a car crash late one night in the desert, he was buried by his family in a three-piece suit. Dan had a Block Island poem about him that bears repeating.

Here Ken Feit disported, who died later.
Command performance, ferry crossing

2. D. Berrigan, *To Dwell in Peace*, 116–17.

> the children crowding round; a clown
> on the ferry! He mimed, cut paper unicorns,
> played on kazoos, combs, jews harp—
> coast to coast. In Stanford chapel, years gone, Feit and I
> made eucharist; he in white face, I in costume
> resplendent. The children ran together
> at his sweet antic tune.
> In wooden pews
> the moody regents muttered woodenly.
> At recessional this was heard:
> 'Could Jesus have seen that, he'd have
> turned over in his grave!'[3]

For a demonstration, Dan once mused poetically on appropriate attire:

> That morning I weighed
> like a Dickens brat
> no expectations. Would I march
> capped in bells like Christ's fool or Christ?
>
> who walked with us
> borne on what wind?[4]

I look at photographs of the Catonsville action and its aftermath. Phil wears a Roman collar, perhaps Daniel too, but I think it is actually a turtleneck with a fish pendant, his formal dress of choice in that period. To be sure the rendering of the brothers on the cover of *Time* shows them in priestly collars and to good effect. They were in the process of dragging the church, kicking and screaming, visibly into the anti-war movement—in much the same way that Martin Luther King, Jr., with his "Beyond Vietnam" speech, was trying mightily to pull the anti-war movement into fuller alignment with the Freedom Struggle and the forces of economic justice. King was doing it as preacher, Dan and Phil liturgically as priests.

Part of Dan's Jesuit formation included a final year, his tertianship, in France, where, among other things, he encountered the worker priest movement. Their pattern was to shed priestly garb entirely and work among laborers, paid and clothed as they. Politically, it represented a move of the

---

3. D. Berrigan, *Block Island,* 37.

4. D. Berrigan, "A Civil Rights Demonstration," in *Risen Bread,* 102.

French church from prominent legitimation of the elite to siding, in that degree, with the working class. Sacramentally, it was an entrance more fully into the world. Dan arrived at the movement's height, a point where priests were becoming involved in labor struggles to the dismay of factory owners. At their behest, the movement was shut down by Pope Pius XII in the very midst of Dan's year in France. (The movement would later be revived in freedom under John XXIII, to whom we shall return.)[5]

I don't mean to linger on apparel and accoutrements, but to say that it seemed to me, for him in priestly matters, such externals were the least of concern, largely to be gone beyond, or deeper.

If Dan was presiding at mass behind ornate and high altars, I was myself never privy to it. Perhaps as a Protestant, it's hard for me to even picture. He certainly despised ecclesial triumphalism and wrote against it. (Too often it went hand in easy hand with warmaking and warmakers in procession.) My experience of his eucharistic touch was more at Catholic Worker houses, living room churches, Jonah House, or his own West Side Jesuit Community circled in a 98th St. apartment. Sacramentally, these were passionate but informal, sometimes improvisational, even rag tag. And yet, or perhaps all the more so, when he uttered the Word and lifted the cup we were rapt in collective mystery. Scenes most ordinary were embraced as most sacred.

I don't know who asked, or even if it was Daniel himself, but he reported that in response to the question of why they celebrated mass so often on the picket line, Cesar Chavez had replied, "I will tell you why. In the first place we are too poor to have parties. In the second place, since we have so few victories, we have to celebrate our defeats."[6] It seemed to me he took both reasons to heart.

Jim Forest tells a lovely story about how when Dan was shepherding the Catholic Peace Fellowship with him and Tom Cornell in New York, they would begin each morning in the office liturgically.

> The style of our eucharistic bread-breaking was as simple and graceful as a Shaker chair and quiet enough to please a Quaker. A prayer for forgiveness was followed by intercessions for friends who were ill or in difficulty. We took turns reading the appointed Old and New Testament texts for the day from a paperback edition of "that old book," the Bible, plus perhaps a supplementary reading

5. Forest, *Lion's Den*, 33–34.
6. Berrigan, "All Honor," 14.

from Neruda or Auden or Peguy or Teilhard, or Brecht, or Merton. After the reading, silence. Then some reflection, usually initiated by Dan, on the readings. More silence. Then a simple canon prayer from the *Bible Missal,* a Mass book widely used at the time. More silence. Finally, after the unspectacular miracle of consecration came the sharing in that quiet miracle, and more silence, perhaps some more prayer, and an embrace at the end.[7]

Somehow this had been surveilled or reported, because they arrived one morning to hear that the informal Eucharist was now officially forbidden. They sat for some time together forlorn and at a loss. Till abruptly, Dan rose, pulled a bottle of wine from the file cabinet, and produced two slices of rye. They did the readings. Silence prevailed instead of a canonical prayer, and Dan finally pronounced a blessing, "Let the Lord make of this what he will." They consumed the feast, hearts satisfied.

Just so. See how similarly Dan describes a Eucharist in the county jail after Catonsville.

I remember also that on the final day we decided to break our fast with a Eucharist. Someone had brought us in a loaf of freshly baked bread. We asked the warden if we might have a bottle of wine. He acceded on the condition that he himself might be present for our Eucharist. Of course, he might. Whereupon, around the board table, began one of the simplest and most moving of communal actions. "Do this in memory of me." Which is to say: "In remembering me, re-member yourselves. Put your lives and souls together again."[8]

Neither walls nor bars nor carceral powers could hold out against the mystery of Christ's communal presence and wholeness.

Knowing that in Christ there is no longer male and female, Dan was an early advocate for women in the priesthood. He wrote of it shortly after the ordination of the first Episcopal women priests, occasioned by his preaching at St. Stephen's and the Incarnation Episcopal Church in DC and being invited to serve communion.

Women who want to enter the priesthood, or who are already ordained, have at least some inkling of the stalemate within the ranks. The truth of being woman is a good boot camp for being a nobody; in culture, in church. And "nobody," "non person" is

7. Forest, *Lion's Den,* 74.

8. Berrigan, *No Bars,* 25.

a good definition of a priest today, female or male, given both church and culture. Properly, soberly understood. Some say the scripture says that's where we belong.

A non person. You don't signify. They look you over, but you don't meet acceptable standards. Or the big boys meet, make big decisions, plans, projections. You aren't invited. Or rather, you're disinvited. World without end.

Priesthood? One could huff and puff about mystery, sacrament, sign, moments of grace. These I take to be realities. I am also consoled that they are out of our grasp, control, consuming . . .

A better beginning might be the common admission of a common plight, male and female, in the effort to be faithful to a human vocation; violation, insults, jail, the beetling brow of the law. Each has the right to kick and scream until we have 1) a common share of our common patrimony (matrimony)—which certainly includes equal access to ministry, pulpit, sacraments, right up to bishoprics and papal tiaras (for those who feel called to such bric-a-brac), and 2) a vote on where and how our lives get lived, used, spent, given.

Access to the mysteries, the good news made both good and new. Need I tell anyone we are being drowned in bad news; certainly bad, hardly new? I think on the contrary, good news waits on women; I think it waits on men. It waits on each of us, reborn.[9]

There is evidence that he struggled with the order and with his orders, but as he once advised me from his own experience with the Jesuits, in my case as pastoral and marital counseling, the important thing was "to stay in the harness."

There was a period where the most notorious modifier of "priest" for him was "fugitive." During his four-month underground sojourn, he held a place on J. Edgar Hoover's Ten Most Wanted list—and did so sacramentally or apostolically—leaving in his wake a patchwork of safe houses. As guest, he had summoned the host, and the hospitality of resistance.

Daniel and the Vietnamese Buddhist monk Thich Nhat Hanh once spoke in essence about the sort of priest Dan was not:

NHAT HANH: Talking of prisoners reminds me of a story of Camus. A prisoner is to be executed in the morning. He is visited by a priest. The prisoner thinks of the priest as living like a dead man, and the prisoner knows he has to work out his own salvation. The chaplain cannot understand him.

9. Berrigan, "Of Priests, Women," 8–10. See also *Ten Commandments*.

BERRIGAN: The priest wants to "help him believe," he says.

NHAT HANH: Yes. The prisoner refuses not because he wants to refuse Christianity. He refuses "salvation" because he knows the priest who has come to see him understands neither himself, nor the man he wants to save.

BERRIGAN: And in that he is quite right, it seems to me. That priest was only interested in some abstract declaration of faith. He came in bad faith, being in the employment of the executioners; and, of course, a prisoner would be sensitive to that if he has any self-respect at all . . . It's intolerable for a priest to lead people to the guillotine and to have the same keys that the guards and the warden have so that he comes and goes freely . . . The priest would have to become a prisoner or something like it. He needs the essential modesty of a prisoner. Then he could test his own formulas of faith, which he is asking the prisoner to believe.[10]

Berrigan speaks here from experience in having his orders measured and tested by the fate and fire of prison. Like Philip, he exercised his priesthood, officially serving mass now and then while imprisoned, though that was only one of many ways he ministered among the prison community. In fact, nurturing community in a place physically and spiritually designed to prevent it would be chief among them.

Daniel certainly exercised priesthood in pastoral acts. I have letters from him that would be essentially characterized as pastoral, words of encouragement, admonition, or care. I only realize in the writing how he was my confessor. I've told more than once how he called me into what was essentially spiritual direction in my seminary days, drawing me out of an inner stuck place. Over time he readily made himself available to my personal crises, and to discernments vocational or actionwise. I've seen him do the same with others. "Don't die," he told someone withering away in despair, "we need you." The guy rose and filled with life, even poetry. He joined actions of nonviolent resistance.

Another friend, Mel Hollander, now of blessed memory, who crashed with our little community at Union Seminary in New York, joined us for Dan's class on Revelation. In our go-round at the beginning, he introduced himself with provocative cynicism, "I'm Mel. I'm dying of cancer." "Gee, that must be exciting," Dan provoked wryly back. It was like a zen whack. Mel too rose and walked—and lived into dying, which took much longer than

---

10. Berrigan and Nhat Hanh, *Raft*, 51–52.

he'd expected. During those years he devoted himself to aiding Vietnamese refugees. In a priestly lifetime, how many souls on this sweet and beset old planet has Berrigan called to life in the gospel? How many sacramental deeds of resurrection? How many hearts so pastorally indebted?

Moreover, for years, Dan was a pastor to the dying, both in a cancer and an AIDS hospice. Especially to the latter, souls often as not rejected outright by family and church, he could offer what used to be called "last rites," but now "anointing the sick," blessing and loving them home.

His nephew, Phil's son Jerry Berrigan, elaborates:

> When AIDS came on the scene, so swift and deadly, he began walking with those who were terminally afflicted. Here of course we're talking mostly about young gay men, in many cases shunned by family, dying in the closet in which they had been made to live. The relationships which grew during his years in this work were transformative for both Dan and his patients; equally important, this work of ally-ship and solidarity stood in rebuke of an intolerant and self-righteous culture. Some would say that he was out in front on the gay-rights issue. He would say that people are essentially good, and that in the breaking of the bread, in the celebrating and grieving and living together, we are all ennobled.[11]

Or think of baptisms—how many namesakes and more did he anoint with water and oil across the movement landscape, sometimes in deep waters or situations of risk?

While in Latin American exile, he wrote home about a baptism in the town of Tacna, Peru, detailing the crush of poverty and burning trash piles there, concluding pointedly, "The bishop . . . wears a train 60 feet long and charges 150 dollars for a wedding in the Cathedral, hardly even speaks on any subject but the evils of communism."[12] Working with a group assisting students serving the poor, he joined a trip to an indigenous community without a priest for liturgy, offering themselves to the task.

> We drove at night into the desert to celebrate Mass in a remote chapel for 25 Indians, mothers + babies and men who work on the railroad at a little pueblo. Quite a scene, but only by candles. One Mother + father brought their baby, a solemn beautiful little guy with eyes like black stars, so I was impounded as godfather. The boy's name which I must put down here with all due solemnity

11. J. Berrigan, "Remembering."
12. Martin, "Conversion," 289.

is ALVARO Quispe Mamani . . . How many Jebs in their flying machines have a godchild in the Peruvian desert?[13]

Once, when he was in Danbury, a Vietnamese couple with a newborn sought permission to visit and have Daniel baptize the child. Communication to him, and the event itself, was prevented by the chaplain in accord with church and prison higher-ups. When he learned about the overture and prohibition later, Dan confronted the priest who equivocated angrily, finally averring, "A prison is no fit place to baptize a child!" Berrigan's anger finally rose to meet his: "You're the type of priest who would have thought that mass should not be celebrated on Calvary!"[14]

Likewise, with funerals or marriages—sacraments made witness to lives marrying justice and peace, in beloved community. I once heard a marriage homily of his that was stunning in its call to resurrection and resistance. Another, his sermon at Stringfellow's funeral, conferred upon Bill a memorable and enduring title: Non-Betrayer, Keeper of the Word.

He preached everywhere. At Worker liturgies, even in prison (though one attempt to circulate a homily of his on paper was aggressively suppressed), as a guest in pulpits large and small, including a notorious underground sermon at a Germantown United Methodist church, videoed and re-circulated. He once preached for me when I was serving part-time in Southwest Detroit. At Preston UMC, in the cavernous sanctuary with a leaking roof, he addressed a smattering of parishioners and the specially notified. It was a scene replicated across the country. A homily once landed him in exile. Forbidden to speak publicly about Roger LaPorte's self-immolation, he addressed LaPorte's New York Worker community at a private mass in an apartment.[15] Yet, in the midst of the war, affirming the young Worker's action not as despair, but as gift and self-sacrifice, sent Berrigan packing for the global south—Mexico, Brazil, Chile, Peru, more.[16] A baptism itself (and whence the baptism story above).

To me it seems that he exercised his priestly vocation broadly in what William Stringfellow called a "sacramental ethic." Witness all said thus far. Nearly everything he did was intended to recognize and reveal the steadfast

13. Martin, "Conversion," 289.

14. Berrigan and Nhat Hanh, *Raft* 54. See another account in D. Berrigan, *Lights on*, 253–254.

15. For the text of that homily see D. Berrigan, "Death Does Not Get the Last Word," in Dear, ed., *Essential*, 65–72.

16. Forest, *Lion's Den*, 91–95.

love beneath all reality. Always and everywhere, he was never not being a priest. But think especially how that vocation transfigured direct action, beginning with Catonsville. As Stringfellow wrote:

> The Berrigan brothers and others of the defendants had been involved over a long time, particularly since the extraordinary papacy of John XXIII, in the renewal of the sacramental witness in the liturgical life of Christians. They had become alert to the social and political implications of the mass . . . [It was] a liturgy transposed from altar or kitchen table to a sidewalk outside a Selective Service Board office, a fusion of the sacramental and the ethical standing within the characteristic biblical witness.[17]

Daniel functioned as street liturgist for Catonsville. Around the burning files he offered prayer:

> May [God] make it possible through this action for others to live. May he make it more difficult for them to kill one another. We make our prayer in the name of that God whose name is peace and decency and unity and love. Amen.[18]

Thereafter he led the group in "The Lord's Prayer." Liturgist, homilist, intercessor.

Sacramental ethic indeed. It's not that Berrigan invented what I've ventured to call "liturgical direct action,"[19] (the Freedom Struggle had its own varieties) but Catonsville did spawn not only a long series of subsequent draft board actions, but an array of analogous public rituals of risk[20]—never mind the subsequent "Plowshares movement"—all bearing the gospel into the streets, in forms rich with meaning.

One precursor in public liturgies familiar to him would stem from the late fifties: the Catholic Worker's six-year resistance campaign against New York City's annual air raid drill, as required by the Civil Defense Act. The drill, compulsory for New Yorkers, was itself precisely a "nuclear liturgy." It socially constructed and maintained the reality of the post-war, cold-war world, and signified the submission of citizens to the bomb's sovereignty in it. Here was a rite in which the young Catholic Workers declined to partake.

---

17. Stringfellow, *Ethic*, 151–52.

18. See footage in Lockwood, dir., *Holy Outlaw*.

19. Wylie-Kellermann, *Seasons*. See also Dear, *Sacrament*.

20. Wylie-Kellermann, "Preface to the 2008 Edition," "Introduction," "Examples Abounding," in *Seasons*, xix–xxvii, 106–12.

At the sound of the siren, they would gather in the streets, each year with more and more support from other pacifist organizations, refusing to take shelter and suffering arrest. Dorothy Day drafted the religious leaflet which declared that one could not have faith in God and depend on the atom bomb at the same time. When, in 1961, 2,000 people joined in public refusal, the compulsory drills simply ceased.

What to make of a "sacramental NO?" Stringfellow referred to the Catonsville action as a "politically informed exorcism."[21] He was not wide of the mark. Exorcism is neither esoteric nor weird. In fact, it is quite commonplace in Christian liturgy. The Lord's Prayer includes an exorcistic plea: Deliver us from evil. And baptism always involves exorcism in the renunciation of Satan and all his works, of the spiritual forces of wickedness, rejecting the evil powers of this world—one way or another.

Dan was once drawn by Stringfellow into a liturgical exorcism of the Block Island house after the passing of Bill's partner, Anthony Towne. Stringfellow employed an ancient liturgy researched and published by the Anglican bishop of Exeter.[22] It was the same text he had used to exorcise Richard Nixon at a Princeton anti-war rally—first to great response and then actually to great effect. Dan recounted the Block Island event autobiographically in some wry detail.

> Under the lash of wind and rain, some fifty friends huddled and endured. According to Stringfellonian decree, liturgies were not to be interrupted by a triviality such as a nor'easter.
>
> The rains turned the book of devotions in my hands to a sopping porridge. It became next to impossible to decode a text fast vanishing. And when the psalms were completed and the ashes laid to rest, we turned with longing toward the shelter of the house, soaked as we were, and shivering with cold.
>
> Not yet. Stringfellow announced in level tones: "Now we shall pause, face the house, and rebuke the principality of death, who has claimed this dwelling."
>
> So instructed, so we did. There followed an exorcism, in the course of which the demon death was, to all intents, banished from the premises. On our watery entrance in the house, there remained no trace of fiery comet, or so much as a blackened hoofprint.
>
> It was all in character. Stringfellow's biblical carefulness allowed for no trivialization of evil, and its secular counterpart,

21. Stringfellow, *Ethic*, 151
22. Petiepierre, ed., *Exorcism.*

the gnostic psychologizing. And because he took the demonic as seriously as did Christ, we are perhaps justified in concluding that Stringfellow also took Christ seriously. In such matters as exorcism, it was evident to him that the integrity of the Gospel was at stake. And that consideration must constrain Christians to linger in inclement weather to perform rituals of moment.[23]

I was once invited for drinks and fresh raw salmon by Bill's neighbor across the road. In the course of conversation, he leaned over to me and confided in hushed tones, "He's an exorcist, you know." Island lore and wisdom freely proffered. And true. Between you and me, Dan is one too.

About the same time as the Island ceremony, Dan wrote of Jesus and the woman bent over (Luke 13):

> In freedom, [Jesus] walks over those puerile taboos and drawn lines. He takes the initiative with the woman; "He called her over when he saw her condition . . ." Then he "laid his hands on her." And simply announced her cure. She straightened up. And "she gave glory to God." How sublime! A woman bent double (bent doubly) under the burden of hideous culture and worse religion, is healed of this evil spirit. For a spirit is at work in her, not a disease; or better, a diseased spirit. The culture, the religion, are rightly regarded by Jesus as demonic. The woman must be exorcised, of culture, or religion. Then she stands upright, then with all her wit and will, she responds to God. Can you see her face at that moment?[24]

An experience comes to mind. Jeanie and I were once part of a Witness for Peace delegation to Nicaragua that accompanied a woman, Juana Francisca, back to her home in the hills, a site filled with terror because her family members had been brutally murdered there. We granted her space for wailing and tears, standing around awkwardly like so many gringos. But we also came prepared with a small service of confession. Readings of Scripture and the Lord's Prayer simultaneously in Spanish and English were followed by a dispersion of blessed water. The young Argentinean priest, who served the parish and its wide circle of base communities was wary at first, eschewing any pretense of magical power or superstition. However, he consented to preside, blessing the water with a simple prayer on behalf of life, and gracefully scattering it upon us all and the site with a branch of

---

23. D. Berrigan, *Dwell*, 257. See also Berrigan's poetic account of the event in *Block Island*, 9–10.

24. D. Berrigan, "Of Priests, Women," 148.

leaves from a sapling by the house. Thus reclaiming the space from death. I
I recounted the event to Dan in a letter:

> We returned with a woman to her home for the first time in over
> a month since the house had been blown open by the Contra, her
> husband [a base community leader] dragged out, knifed open, and
> his heart cut out. She wailed and wept, hard to know if (once we got
> her there encouraged and safely) we were more gift or intrusion on
> sacred grief. We prayed with her at the cross-marked spot. Sang.
> Read Romans 8. Stringfellow would have called it an exorcism.[25]

Comparative exorcistic events might be sampled. Let me suggest one
exemplar of note. Cheryl Kirk-Duggan has marshalled a substantial Womanist analysis of the Black Spirituals, and called it *Exorcising Evil*.[26] Her own
pilgrimage in the terrain she counted "a sacramental worship experience."
Personally for her, the Spirituals, those songs created by African American
slaves and eventually reworked by civil rights activists, "affirm God and cope
with oppression, anchor my soul, awaken history for me, and reflect a significant portion of my life."[27] She essentially points to them as a body of liturgical
action that disempowers the demonic of slavery and white male supremacy,
and opens human space for Black lives. Taking Jesus seriously.

Dan Berrigan once acted a priest in a motion picture, *The Mission*.[28]
Though his was a minor part, portraying an elder Jesuit priest in eighteenth-
century Paraguay, he verily seemed to depict himself. He also served as a
consultant to the film about the Vatican-supported incursion of slavery into
the region. Because the Jesuits resisted, in support of the indigenous community, they were effectively shut down as an order for decades. Though
the film is built around that history, his advice and suggestion figured into
various scenes and characters and especially the denouement of the film. As
the slavers attack the utopian spiritual and economic compound, certain of
the Jesuits take to arms in support. In the original script, the lead Jesuit who
refuses violence, was to celebrate mass as the blazing walls of the mission
collapse upon him and his indigenous congregation. Dan's advice: why not
instead have him walk out toward the attackers, the Eucharist held visible
and high in hand, with the congregation behind him. Before the holy sight,

---

25. Copy of handwritten letter of the author to Daniel Berrigan, February 18, 1986.
Author's files.

26. Kirk-Duggan, *Exorcising Evil*.

27. Kirk-Duggan, *Exorcising Evil*, xv.

28. See Film Presence Aside to chapter 10.

the soldiers hesitate, forced under orders to choose. He is struck down, like Romero at the altar, but not as a silent victim. Not in liturgical passivity, but in the boldness of sacramental action, walking in nonviolent holiness. It is sufficient to serve here as image of his priestliness.

During my last visit with Dan, at Fordham's Murray-Weigel Hall, we attended mass together in the Jesuit infirmary's small chapel. He led the way, but I was pushing him in a wheelchair. Behind a stone altar, another aged celebrant was resplendent, fully vested, in a chasuble. (I did wonder had Dan himself served here and vested so in recent past.) At the consecration, a room full of hands, including Dan's, reached toward the host in love and authority—and again when he received, open handedly. A priest indeed, always and to the end.

Homiletic Aside: A Berrigan Wedding Sermon

(In the spring of 1975 I presided at the marriage of two
friends in James Chapel at Union Theological Seminary.
Dan preached. I assisted at communion. What follows is a
transcription of his remarks.)

Dear Friends,

All those who are gathered to rejoice and share this day:

I want to begin with a text that does not mean to pre-empt the beautiful words of Scripture and the words of song already spoken and sung, but rather to complement them.

From a message of the Vietnamese people to certain friends in the West, recently sent:

> We have a saying in Vietnamese when a very difficult thing is to
> be done. It is like trying to break a rock with an egg. And indeed
> in these days the Vietnamese people have shown that they are able
> to do this most difficult thing. For after twelve to fifteen years of
> bloodletting, the Vietnamese egg is unbroken and the American
> rock is severely damaged. And we say to all our friends in the
> West: Whatever you do for us is more valuable than gold. To write,
> to speak the truth, to stand somewhere, to speak for the victims,
> and come to our help; all this is much more than if you would pour
> your wealth upon us.

Truly, dear friends, our young friends this morning have decided to break a rock with an egg. And so all sorts of rhythms have been set in motion by this most unexpected act. An act which seems so in accord with nature as to be almost against nature. That is to say, against the rock which is speechless, and the rock which has no future, they have set this unborn egg, teeming with future, teeming with hope, containing all their tomorrows. And having decided to enter into that covenant which is also a conflict between the forces of death and the unborn, they have gathered us in order to read there also a most unlikely thing, which is to say: tomorrow is possible. And not any tomorrow at all, not a tomorrow which depends on the victory of the rock, the victory of brute power which claims the world and our own soul, but an entire turn around, an ironic twist, a vindication of nature and grace. Which is to say, the egg will remain unbroken, and shall break in God's good time. And there shall issue forth from it, the living. And on that day we shall know it is not necessary that the blood of those we have chosen to hate is necessary to anoint our entrance.

In the last bloody decade every time we have had a wedding it is because we have been facing a new crisis. And the converse is true: every time we were facing a new crisis, in God's providence, we had a wedding. And that was because the one was inevitable, and the other was of Grace. The one was because we were trying to live in the world as though we contained the future, and the other was because God came to say Yes to that vision of things. And in the moment of the wedding we took courage again to live in the world and needed to pause and eat and drink and celebrate that life which was asking so much from us. And so those rhythms which seemed so contrary became a reaching out and a grasping of one another. And the complement was strong, containing for its very richness all the oppositions of no and yes, of death and life, of fear and hope, of despair common to all flesh, and of joy most uncommon to our lives.

Every time the rock beat above us and threatened our existence, we were able to set against it the egg of the resurrection. Every time the rock claimed for us every species of human dwelling, claiming to be able to rubble, and indeed showed most brutally that power in the world, we were able to set against it the simple hope of those who set against hate, love. Of those who set against duplicity, simplicity and truth. Of those who set against violence, the deliberate choice to cherish and nurture one another. And so in the midst of war a few make peace. And in the midst of death, a few make love. And that makes all the difference.

And so we are still on our feet as a deathly Watergate supplies a filthy continuity with the death in South Vietnam. We are still on our feet. We are still passing bread and wine to one another. We are still setting against the rock, the egg which is not crushed.

We say thank you to these two, who in a desperate and perplexing time, do so unlikely and lovely a thing.

— Chapter 5 —

Poet: Of the Word Incarnate[1]

You are jail-yard blooms,
You wear bravery with a difference.
You are born here will die here;
Making you, by excess of suffering
And transfiguration of suffering, ours.

Between life as fools pace
and life as celebrant's flame—aeons.
Yet, thank you. Against the whips
Of ignorant furies, the slavish pieties of judas priests
You stand, a first flicker in the brain's soil, the precursor
Of judgement.
Dawn might be, we may be
Or
Spelling it out in the hand's palm
Of a blind mute

God is fire, is love[2]

With permanent marker, in his distinctive (even calligraphic) hand, Daniel Berrigan, poet and priest, covered the dining room wall of our little hospitality and resistance house in Battle Creek with this portion of "Tulips in the Prison Yard." It was a blessing and virtually a call to discipleship. The house and wall are gone altogether, but still I know the poem by heart.

1. Wylie-Kellermann, "Daniel Berrigan."
2. A portion of D. Berrigan, "Tulips in the Prison Yard," in *Prison Poems,* 23–24.

The poem stems from his own imprisonment for burning draft files in Catonsville, Maryland as a protest in 1968 against the war in Vietnam. The nonviolent direct action by nine Catholics was distinctive for implicating the church in the anti-war movement, but even moreso for casting the action in the poetics of liturgy. It took direct action to another discipline and dimension—of word and spirit.

Dan drafted—what to even call it, a press release? action statement? movement missive? in language to become a masterpiece of spiritual/political/poetic writing. A portion here:

> . . . There we shall of purpose and forethought
> remove the 1-A files sprinkle them in the public street
> with home-made napalm and set them afire
> For which act we shall beyond doubt
> be placed behind bars for some portion of our natural lives
> in consequence of our inability
> to live and die content in the plagued city
> to say "peace peace" when there is no peace
> to keep the poor poor
> the thirsty and hungry thirsty and hungry.
> Our apologies, good friends,
> for the fracture of good order, the burning of paper
> instead of children, the angering of the orderlies
> in the front parlor of the charnel house
> We could not so help us God do otherwise
> For we are sick at heart. Our hearts
> give us no rest for thinking of the Land of Burning Children . . . [3]

Dan's testimony at the federal trial reiterated the statement, but more to the point, the trial was altogether one with the moral and poetic trajectory of the action. The jury may have convicted the Nine, but Daniel published the court transcript of their testimonies, with pertinent prose quotations inserted, almost like choruses (Camus, Brecht, Neruda, Fidel, Ho Chi Minh), as a play in free verse that has been produced internationally and filmed, and which is, at this writing, in revival on a New York stage. It is set before another jury of conscience: ourselves.

---

3. Dear, ed., *Essential*, 105–6.

Berrigan's testimony in the dock recounted how he came, step by step, in conversion of conscience to Catonsville. Two events were most excruciating and immediate. One was the anti-war self-immolation of a young man in Syracuse, whom Dan visited in the hospital room before his death (see his discussion on this topic with Thich Nhat Hanh in *The Raft Is Not the Shore*.) The other, in Hanoi to retrieve captured American soldiers, he crouched in a bomb shelter beneath the onslaught of US B-52s. In fact, the last words of the defense summation to the jury are another poem of Dan's telling that moment with "children in the shelter."

> I picked up the littlest
> a boy, his face
> breaded with rice (his sister calmly feeding him
> as we climbed down)

> In my arms fathered
> in a moment's grace, the messiah
> of all my tears. I bore, reborn
> a Hiroshima child from hell.[4]

Members of the jury, what say you?

While awaiting an appeal, Daniel Berrigan read and reviewed Eldridge Cleaver's *Soul on Ice*.[5] He was struck by the "new language" the Black Panther invented in prison, refusing the method those in power call "civilized discourse"—"adopted almost universally by the little gray men in glasses who make the decisions about the many who shall die and the few who shall live, from Harlem to Hanoi." Resistance required a new idiom, a shift in the very elementals of thought and speech. Cleaver's new method "has something to do with the soil in which the mind of man grows. The soil today is stony indeed, a combination of prison rock, macadam, ennui, unreason, enclosure, the stifling threat of violence, mindlessness. No matter. What we are talking about is prophetic discourse, fury in the face of repression . . . "[6]

Was it a self-conscious preparation for his own pending prison discourse? Perhaps. But first a poet's interlude. Berrigan declined to submit himself for prison, slipping away in front of US Marshals at a public event,

4. Dear, ed., *Essential*, from "Children in the Shelter," 101–2.

5. Cleaver, *Soul*.

6. D. Berrigan, "This Man is Armed," *No Bars*, 150.

onstage slipping into an eight-foot effigy, a giant puppet of a disciple (see further chapter 9). You can't make this stuff up. For five months he haunted the nation underground—harbored, preaching, interviewed on national television, corresponding publicly and writing poetry from J. Edgar Hoover's Ten Most Wanted list.

Beginning on the "Feast of Bonhoeffer," he composed six pages of verse on Eberhardt Bethge's then-new biography, for *The Saturday Review*. They began:

> I begin these notes on 9 April 1970. Two hours ago, at 8:30 A.M.,
> I became a fugitive from injustice, having disobeyed
> a federal court order to begin
> a three-year sentence for destruction of draft files two years ago.
> It is the twenty-fifth anniversary of the death of Dietrich Bonhoeffer
> in Flossenburg prison, for resistance to Hitler.
> The temperature outside is 64. It is a foggy, wind-driven day
> well tempered to my mood
> But let me begin at the beginning.
> My theme, as Bonhoeffer would put it, is faith and obedience.
> He said: **Invisibility breaks us to pieces.** Again:
> **Simply suffering; that is what will be needed—not parries or blows**
> **or thrusts. The real struggle which perhaps lies ahead**
> **must consist only in suffering belief.**
> And again: **The task is not only to bind up the victims beneath**
> **the wheel, but also to put a spoke in that wheel . . .** [7] (Emphasis Dan's.)

By August, exhausted and hoping for some quiet days to sit still, to talk and write, he was arrested by the FBI, posing infamously as birdwatchers, at the Block Island home of William Stringfellow and Anthony Towne. He would recall,

> *How's this for a time warp?*
> Year's gone, the maladroit
> Malodorous bird watchers poked about. I sat in the yard
> Storms gathering, slicing country apples.
> They pounced, the bird was nabbed!
> That scene, domestic, hilarious, once & for all foreclosed.
> Bill gathered the remnants, that nothing be lost.
> Two years went by; then
> Return of the native!

7. See D. Berrigan, "The Passion of Dietrich Bonhoeffer," in *America*, 39.

> Welcome, spectacular banquet;
>
> Dessert? Resurrected apples,
>
> Deep dish pie![8]

Resurrection was an experience of his prison time (Stringfellow re-remarked on this freedom of Dan and Phil during a visit in 1970). Most explicit in this regard is "The Risen Tin Can." At the back of Danbury Federal Correctional Institution Berrigan observed and heard a machine for crushing flat the metal refuse of the kitchen. It struck him as a stand-in for the very function of the place upon its inhabitants. Here but a glimpse:

> We prisoners are, so to speak, tin cans
> emptied of surprise, color, seed, heartbeat, pity, pitch, frenzy
> molasses, nails, ecstasy, etc., etc.
> destined to be whiffed and tumbled into elements of flatland
> recycled, dead men's bones, dead souls—
> Now the opposite of all this is the shudder and drumming feet
> of the risen tin can
> over the hill, into the sunrise
> The tin can contains, grows wings, he writes poetry!

> This is the year of the RISEN TIN CAN, in the Vietnamese sense.
> REVOLUTION REFUSAL REBUTTAL POETRY.
> When I was a tin can I thought like a tin can I looked like a tin can
> I spoke like a tin can
> now that I am a man I have put away the things of a tin can
> *nempe*
> tin armaments tin hearts tin bells rin-tin-tin gross national tin
> American tin . . . .
>> The unforgiveable sin against the unholy spirit
>> is the metamorphosis of tin into manhood.
> Of which one instance: the writing of a poem . . .[9]

As Dan told Jim Forest, his friend and now biographer, "I should have gone to prison sooner. It's a pressure cooker of poetry."[10]

---

8. D. Berrigan, *Block Island*, 17.

9. "The Risen Tin Can," D. Berrigan, *Prison Poems* 32, 33. I have framed on my study wall a crushed and rusted tin can. It was a gift with the poem in mind.

10. Forest, *Lion's Den*, 153.

Dan won poetry awards for his early work, but truly some of his best originated in trial, on the run, and in the lockup. Kurt Vonnegut once quipped, "For me, Daniel Berrigan is Jesus as poet." (I want to think as a parable writer; Jesus actually did all right for himself in that regard.)

For Berrigan, poetry was mode and method of survival. He once recounted that the homilies of the Danbury prison chaplains were so deadly and mind-numbing that he took up the discipline of memorizing T. S. Eliot's *Four Quartets* during sermon time at mass. Focusing and clarifying the mind. Upon release he came to New York City to teach a course on the Revelation of John. As students, we could hear the echoes of Eliot in his reading of apocalypse . . . where "in the end is our beginning."

For my money his best poem from prison is long and little known. "A Letter to Vietnamese Prisoners" was published by the Merton Center in New York City, with art by fellow prisoner, Tom Lewis. I've no doubt it was delivered to its intended by way of Nhat Hanh, then exiled in Paris. During the Tiger Cage Fast and Vigil in the summer of 1974, taking a page from Dan, I committed the entire poem to memory while sitting inside a mock tiger cage cell, used for political prisoners in Vietnam, on the steps of the US Capitol. With a little refreshment or prompting I can recite the poem still. Here just its beginning and its end.

> Dear friends, your faces are a constriction of grief in the throat
> your words weigh us like chains, your tears and blood
> fall on our faces. Prison; Vietnam, prison; U.S.
> prison is our fate, mothers bear us in prison,
> our tongues taste its gall, bars spring up
> from dragons' teeth, a paling, impaling us.
> A universal malevolent will, crouched like a demon
> blows winter upon us, stiffens our limbs in death, the limbs of
> women and children . . .
>
> It is snowing tonight as I vigil.
> The first white fall of winter
> bitterly cold. I think on
> the fevers and horrors of Con Son.
>
> No their No. YES to all else.[11]

---

11. Berrigan, *Vietnamese Letter*, 1, 7.

Revelrous Aside: Bad Parenting Story for Comedic Relief

It must have been August, 1991. The Sojourners had put on a conference about faith and social justice. The venue was Calvin College, a Christian Reformed Church institution in Grand Rapids, Michigan. I should say up front that it was, by rule, a "dry campus."

Dan was one of the speakers for the week, reading poetry and giving conversational workshops on resistance. One day, word was spread that he was hosting a gathering in his dorm room that evening. My beloved partner, Jeanie, and I sorely wanted to attend, but we had in tow our five-year-old daughter, Lydia. Past her bedtime.

We had along what was then called a "baby minder," a small one-way radio for broadcasting a baby's cries to another part of the house to alert listening parents. Dan's room was only a short distance across a courtyard. We tested it. What could go wrong? Against the chance of malfunction, we taped a note on the door: "If the child cries, we are in room such and such."

The party was wonderful, lubricated with plenteous smuggled cases of beer and some scotch. (My friend Ched Myers reminds me that he was Dan's roommate and booze smuggler for the event). Conversations were picked up or launched, jokes (with impeccably timed punchlines) were bantered back and forth. Ed Spivey, art and layout editor for *Sojourners*, whose real vocation is stand-up comic, was in finest fettle spoofing events of the week. I'd just begun talking with Robert Ellsberg, then newly editor at Orbis and reviewing a manuscript from me, when a knock came on the door. Upon opening, there stood a security guard hand in hand with Lydia. Silence descended upon the room. Says Lydia: "Why did you leave me a note when you know I can't read?" Robert, then an expectant father, blanched. Says the security guy, coolly surveying the room: "Get it out of here." The party was over. (Or, so far as I know, moved elsewhere.)

— Chapter 6 —

Prisoner: Letter on the Glass of a Wall

Dear Bill—

I'm sitting here giving thanks for you, winging thoughts & prayers your way, getting ready to MAKE DINNER FOR A FEW UNAT-TACHED (sorry caps) or detached friends. But above all simply to say thank you on the west wind, hoping my prayer like a wayward feather or a beam of light, comes home to yer durance. Keeping at it is the word for the times. T.y. for keeping at it . . .

The cross [reverse] is from an old book, composed in Danbury; Jesus Christ. I found it and sed to myself, maybe it'll make the moon come up . . . I'm sorry Jeanie is taking yr. stay so hard; but she has good sense and substance, and things will go better . . . I'm sending a poem or two. Culhane is a lifer at Sing Sing. The other poet, otherwise known to you, is, I suppose, also thought of as a lifer. At least he aint a deather.

My love through the iron, Daniel[1]

(What follows is a seminary paper from my studies at Union Theological Seminary in 1975 for a class offered by Tom Driver on Poetry and Theology. Berrigan's prison poem "Vietnamese Letter," on which it is based, follows as an "Epic Aside." I believe the letter poem, though little known, is substantial and significant. My commentary reflects a youthful passion and sober exuberance. A formation in process. I include it here for that reason as well.)

---

1. D. Berrigan to the author in Bay County Jail, dated "Thanksgiving," author's files.

Prologue

Do not read this letter to the Vietnamese if you cling to your life, but have eyes and ears for the sacred metaphors of Jeremiah, Jesus, or John the Divine. Or even the Buddha. If you swallow it whole, it explodes in your guts and comes pouring out of your life in flames. Or perhaps creeps slowly until just when you're about to grab hold of it, to find that it has hold of you, staking its bloody claim. A warning, do you hear?

I have come to know it by heart. The piece meal of meditation's days. "By heart" when we're asked to do so much by head; "by memory" when practice is everywhere to forget. It echoes in me here and there, now and then, like the fall of a distant hammer. Do you know?

It is, Dear Friends, a letter. Sacramental common meal of the word. Transcendent form in your eye. Sender and Receiver implied almost in every word, with a concrete presence which resists dissolution or abstraction. Both absent ones are present to the "other" and so to us. Do you see?

Between us and the Vietnamese, a wall: systematic lie, military and political; amnesia induced out of sight and mind and heart; the fiery metal technology of death (they below, the dying—we above the falling). But here, in truth, is a chink. The wall is a door. Imagine! Lord and servant of time and space. Someone gets connected through it all. Like Paul tells the Corinthians: you are a letter from Christ written on your heart. Do you get it?

When Daniel Berrigan entered Danbury Federal Prison in 1970 for the burning of draft files at Catonsville, Maryland, a religious journal lamenting the fact editorially hoped he would be free soon and able to resume his priestly duties. It would be just as absurd to hope him soon free to write poetry once again. In fact, he'd merely been "appointed Laureat in Residence at the Imperial Madhouse, Woebegone Acres." Neither his orders nor his poetic license had been suspended. And those two offices not only come together, but are virtually inseparable in "Letter to the Vietnamese."

Part 1

Journey Toward: Face to Face

I imagine that this poem ducked the censor's hand at Danbury; no mail room examinations. Let us guess it was passed hand to hand, concealed in the kiss of peace at the close of a service, then out the visitor's door in this friend's pocket. Air mail to Paris, the Buddhist Peace Delegation, joyfully received and translated. By whom? Thich Nhat Hanh himself? Commended again to the mails, more planes—and so variously to Saigon. From there copies scatter outward.

Berrigan wrote early, "The poem/ is the journey toward."[2] That is perhaps true of this one more than any other. It is intended for its subject. It goes to those whom we thereby recall: the 200,000 civilian political prisoners still held in the jails of Saigon. More to the concrete, I have been trying to remember Vo Than Luc, charged with civil disobedience, and the Venerable Le Can, a Buddhist monk, one of those moved from Chi Hoa prison to somewhere in the "military zone" after taking part in the month-long water fast. I bore each of their names, representing each of them in public vigils of disobedience. This letter carries me toward them as well.

It is hoped we come very close. The first sentence begins with "your faces" and ends with "our faces." Mirroring one another. If we can see them, we'll find their tears upon our cheeks.

Perhaps in reading, the Vietnamese will find also themselves reflected. The poem literally echoes the first line from one by Nhat Hanh himself, "Fires spring from dragon's teeth up at the ten points of the universe."[3]

Landscape: Deathly Cold

The power of death covers everything, not so much as fire, but as ice and snow, bitterly cold (line 172). Even Christ would languish on ice (128). Winter. You can feel it in Berrigan's bones. Forgetful snow. But perhaps Christmas is coming? At any rate we're going shopping, off to the marketplace (10–16). The catalogue is well marked, but the price is high—everything inflated with death. For sale: slaughtered flesh, ground flat—their bones to make our bread (153); military hardware (12); the hammer of mad bombers (40). Can we no longer see through the greed of the jeweler's glass? (13) Death is disguised and displayed and packaged, coated sweet as honey. It is shouted and blared and made normal as everyday until we are left standing, numb and cold, packages under arm. We have purchased death, consumed

---

2. I have been unable to locate a citation for this quote in a forty-five-year-old student paper. I let it stand as is.

3. Nhat Hanh, "Our Green Garden," in Nhat Hanh and Vo-Dinh, *Cry,* 34.

and devoured it, swallowed it wide-eyed and more. We might not see the dragon's teeth but have surely become its belly.

Out of Sight and Mind (and Heart): Obscene Space (17)

No Bars to Manhood: "Blood was let, the tragedies were steeped in blood. But such action was strictly, from a dramatic point of view obscene; *Ob scaenum,* banished, forbidden the stage, such abominations, such shady business, could only occur off stage, somewhere in the wings."[4]

Prison as Metaphor: Wall, Mirror, Window

(somewhere in the wings)

The images of lines 17–26 are perhaps the sharpest and most compacted of the poem, wanting to burst or burst out like a moon held underground. These seem to be in part a "midrash" of sorts from a poem of Thomas Merton's. Compare these lines from "The Moslem's Angel of Death":

Like a jeweled peacock he stirs all over
With fireflies. He takes pleasure in
Lights.
He is a great honeycomb of shining bees
Knowing every dust with sugar in it.
He has a million fueled eyes . . .

He turns the city lights in his hand like money . . .

He is a miser. His fingers find the money.
He puts the golden lights in his pockets . . .[5]

These images are of the death's reign in the City, while Berrigan reworks these and more to speak of prison. The connection is clue for movement in the other direction. Quite simply, prison is the city, the culture up close. It is the logical extension, the threat hidden (or not so hidden) behind every

4. D. Berrigan, *No Bars*, 69.
5. Merton, "The Moslem's Angel of Death," *Selected Poems*, 104–5.

law, the form of power which exacts every demand for silence or complicity. Prison itself is the image. House of the dead. To look on prison walls is to see reflected the life or lifelessness of our culture. Prison is a metaphor of our culture, maybe the best one; a metaphor of death.

The program of death is cloture. Narrowing down, all possible alternatives excluded, to the final "definitive solutions." Prison narrows "time" served, nailing shut days and moments like coffins. Prison narrows space—living in a cell. The project is to deny room for dignity, compassion, community . . . I think on how those recent letters from Vietnam report that the place of the tiger cages on Con Son has been usurped by things more deathly: the tiger caves. People can only sit or lie with legs folded because the space is so small. The policy of the administration to regulate not only food and water, but light and air as well. (It is said the cigarettes of the guards go out for lack of oxygen.) Closure. Squeezing life in a strangle hold. Snuffing it out.

But Berrigan's images proclaim even in prison you may nurture that endangered flame (159). Something will not be contained. Fish dart about even in the darkest water (18), eyes in tiger cages flash back to us (19), and that Buddhist moon patiently endures throttling (22), but it yet will rise.

In part 5, the poet confesses, "It's hard in America, hard/ even in American prison/ to take death seriously" (139–41). Would it be easier to go to Vietnam and crouch in a shelter beneath the bombs? Perhaps. But prison seems to be a further step in the same direction. A paradox: to travel to the farthest forgotten edge of the empire where the bombs rain down, or to journey inward into the bowels, is to arrive in the same place: standing with the victims beneath the nailed boot (24). Foreign domestic policies, idem. (165). The machine yields a single fate. "Beyond it all . . . " (17), he says, "you and I" (23). Beneath the nailed boot, we find our eyes and see one another. Walls, and space, and power being no barrier at all.

Part 2

Imagination: Advent and Apocalypse

I recall that prison as a metaphor occurred to Bonhoeffer at least once. He thought it might be compared to Advent—waiting and hoping, not very much to be "done." "The door is closed and locked and can only be opened from the outside."[6]

> If I were free! the phrase flies from our minds
> like a two edged sword, an apocalypse cutting us free[7]

Apocalypse: shearing vision. Precisely a severing off, a radical break within history (jail break?), a cutting—the strings of power fall and the puppet slumps (53).[8] An ending, a closing of the age which is really an opening, an unsealing of the door. The universe is reborn: flesh and family and tribe and nation all things made new! (70–71). See: he comes, the end who is the beginning.

If I were free. The possibility which breaks the best engineered cloture. It is the event, I want to say advent, of imagination. Stuck inside the concrete metaphor of prison, where survival is the preoccupation, it surely must come hard. But it comes. A gift of the spirit. And where the spirit is, there is freedom.

Resistance as eggshell (40)

From a message of the Vietnamese people to certain friends in the West, recently sent:

> We have a saying in Vietnamese when a very difficult thing is to be done. It is like trying to break a rock with an egg. And indeed these days the Vietnamese people have shown that they are able to do this most difficult thing. For after twelve to fifteen years of bloodletting, the Vietnamese egg is unbroken and the American rock is severely damaged. And we say to all our friends in the West: Whatever you do for us is more valuable than jewels or gold. To write, to speak the truth, to stand somewhere, to speak for the victims, and come to our help; all this is much more than if you would pour your wealth upon us.[9]

Against the rock of prison walls, the hammering rock of bombers, set this fragile shelter of the unborn, teeming with life: imagine tomorrow.

---

6. Bonhoeffer, "Letter to Eberhard Bethge," *Letters and Papers*, 96.

7. D. Berrigan, *Vietnamese Letter*, 2.

8. Here and following, parenthetical numbers denote line numbers of the poem.

9. See above, p. 65.

Reconciliation, Between You and Me:
Imagine the Real World

Two words of the Vietnamese come up again into the heart. Their definition of that reconciliation is that transcendent vision which sees two sides
of the conflict as part of the same reality. I am thinking of the dramatic ink
drawings of Vietnamese artist, Vo-Dinh. I've meditated on two of his images side by side—Brothers and Brothers II.[10] In the first, two human forms
arise as part of the single tree trunk with roots in earth. They turn on one
another in rage armed with knives to strike simultaneously. It's a horror.
The second shows a monk sitting in lotus position as a tank, this flying rage
of metal and machine, bears down upon him. Clearly a brother hidden inside is imagined. This art is in the service of the Buddhist campaign, "Don't
Shoot Your Own Brother." Nhat Hanh held that people were shooting at
labels and killing their sisters and brothers.

In a certain reversal, Berrigan is inside the machine looking out and
has dared to recognize brothers and sisters. To put the brake on the machine.
He is proclaiming what they say no one knows any more beyond their own
skin: reality. Here, he says, is something you can sink your dragon's teeth
into: invisible suffering people are real. That is a gift of imagination. What,
in an earlier version of the poem, were its very last lines:

> It is snowing tonight as I vigil
> The first white fall of winter,
> bitterly cold. I think on
> the fevers and horrors of Con Son.

He imagines the real world. A world of lives at least as real as the
forgetful snow. "Between you and me . . . between those hands . . . nothing,
nothing is lost" (31–37). He proclaims good news: the reality of reconciliation and the reconciliation of reality. As though of this he were convinced:
that neither life nor death, nor time nor space, nor ideologies, nor governments, nor prison walls, can separate us.

> they live in us, the lords and servants of time
> we live in them, the lords and servants of time (59–60).

Bonhoeffer speaks of intercession almost as imagination. "His need
and his sin become so heavy and oppressive that we feel them as our own,

---

10. Nhat Hanh and Vo-Dinh, *Cry*, 16, 17.

and we can do nothing else but pray."[11] Our brother's or sister's own prayer, and for their sake. By the lord and servant of imagination, we bear them in our flesh like broken bread.

Lines 59–71 tell of a common meal of reconciliation, a promised banquet. Thich Nhat Hanh has reported that on a visit to the Paris Peace Delegation, Berrigan recently shared a eucharist with the Vietnamese Buddhists. I think it is not so heretical to suggest that in this letter he had already done so. Priestly, poetic, and prison duties being one.

Part 3

Synonyms: Imagine and Believe

The movement from the "if" of line 27 toward the "shall" of line 50, is found repeated in part 3 of the poem. These "antonyms" are a contemporary "beatitudes" of sort. Sprung between "that day" and "but first" is a tension called a promise. A promise that Berrigan does not offer as saccharine comfort to distant wounds, but a promise, I think, he stakes his life upon. He would cite Martin Buber for the connection of belief to imagination. Belief: absurd conviction of things not seen. Will you dare to imagine that day?

Part 4

Crucifixion as Amnesia: How is the Coming Generation to Live?

This little parable reads like the fulfillment of the "but first" prophecies, though its reality is only bearable in the light of the promised day. I made the mistake once of reading only the story in a worship gathering, apart from the preceding section. A deadening silence.

It seems to be about the breakdown of community (like prison firsthand), a story of the fall, about how the reconciliation of reality comes to be forgotten. Of how the meal of promise is violated by degrees. For time and space in the story (here or there, now or then) read: human consciousness, read: the human heart. Time, here, the years of a generation. Space is no room, no house, no distance, but the relation of people and truth. Time and history are the generation of human consciousness, spiraling outward in

11. Bonhoeffer, *Life Together*, 88.

widening gyre, unleashed and unsealed, away from one another and from the true center. The farthest is a horror. Absolute forgetfulness and murderous blindness. The rule of death. And here is the real horror: we are there under that rule. Remember me until I come.

Slaughter of Innocents:
Messiah of All My Tears

Bonhoeffer: "that Christ was born in a stable because there was no room for him in the inn—these are things which a prisoner can understand better than anyone else."[12]

Begin anew. Behold, he comes. It is, as things turn out, Christmas (lines 100–110). The birth of a child—do you imagine his mother bearing him in prison? (4). Lamps of the universe have been seen in the east, a season is decorated and "wreathed" with smiles. This is more than establishing "time and place." History is to be done also with another parable; that special and true story: the Christian year, story of whom the Gospel poets speak.

But the rhythm turns again. Continual counterpoint. Joy and promise serve to reveal the horror once more. Already mangers feel of crosses; already soldiers of the king murder innocents like babes.

In Hanoi in 1968, crouched in a shelter beneath the bombs of B-52s, Daniel Berrigan hefted a child into his arms.

> In my arms fathered
> in a moments grace, the messiah
> of all my tears. I bore reborn
> a Hiroshima child from Hell.[13]

We need a foreign policy for the children (156) or at least an ethic for the children. If good women and men, by saying No with their lives cannot succeed in turning back the future of insanity, then they must at least with their lives "go on record" for those unborn. In a bad time, signs of sane conduct (120) and compassion (123) must endure.

---

12. Bonhoeffer, *Letters and Papers from Prison,* 166.
13. D. Berrigan, *Risen Bread,* 114.

Imagination and Incarnation:
the Poet as Poem

The Poet to Himself

Color it not kind
with skies of love and amber:
make it plain with death
and bitter as remember.

You who set easel
to sigh by willows—
your lie will lie
tomorrow with mildews.

but yours no shutterblink
transfer of view:
your paint be blood
your canvas you.[14]

When history is demythologized, de-mystified, unmasked, rendered recognizable, by the Christian year and the Gospel story; when history is understood as drama, powers summoned to the stage of human consciousness and set in conflict, the task of ethics, sane conduct, human living becomes to enter that drama in the name, let us say, of Buddha or Christ. Not that one constructs himself as a character, but is led by imagination into their infinite ways.

Perhaps enough is already said, or at least implied, of all this in "prison as metaphor." But the poet does not simply look around, being today, as it happens, in prison and say, "Aha, walls and death and snow reveal . . ." No. He walked into it, he puts it on like a garment, filling, with a pound of his own flesh, the pen drawn lines. The *prisoner* is the metaphor: American conscience sealed in concrete and steel, but still a sign of hope.

Something bold: it is the brief account of Catonsville (110–15) which brings all of this to mind. In the face of cruelty, conceive an ironic twist: burn paper instead of children. This is far more than poetry as press release. It is true liturgy: the public work, imagination of alternatives. Sign. A signature, one might hope, on the same line with God's signature in Christ.

14. D. Berrigan, "The Poet to Himself," in *Time*, 4.

Ethics as sacrament, sacrament as politics, politics as confession of faith, credo as event. The word is: make it flesh.

Something simple: I think of Thich Nhat Hanh washing his hands and so raising a thought which goes well with the washing of hands: that the world be cleaned and purified. Here is the simplest event of daily life become a contemplative act, an occasion for meditation. In the "Letter," I think of these lines, "stiffens our limbs in death, the limbs of woman and children" (9), or again, "wreathe in smiles our stiff jointed discontent" (105). What I hear, in part, is the pain of arthritis aggravated by a prison cold winter. The stuff of one's life as metaphor. A transformation. Each touch of pain sparks the imagination of suffering, the memory of what others endure. This is not the inflation of mock heroism (132), but a private contemplative event. Make your life the poem, as the poem your life.

Befouling Apes: Messianic Parody

That the stigma of Cain should be burned on the forehead of Abel (115) is a dramatic reversal of the right order. Here the mark of baptism, Paul's "stigma" is usurped as the "mark of the beast." That mark? A claim worn in many ways: the draft card mark of assent carried on the left butt of one's ass, income tax forms, credit card, credentials, security—all more of the same.

The mimicry or aping of mark for mark, blasphemy for truth, is a plague. It is called in the poem as mock-heroism and mock-victimhood (133). It is there in the legions who claim *messianic* (146) to kill a commie for any ideology whatever. It is even there in the jeweler's glass (24), a paste imitation of Buddha's evening star.

It is all to be expected, almost counted upon. But wrong order is occasion for choice—and there we go again.

Liquid Fire and Frozen Hard Heart

American airmen dropping their liquid fire (169). I cannot read the line without seeing vividly the opening footage of the film *Year of the Tiger*. It is several minutes of Air Force-shot, Kodacolor realism, wide-eyed view of bombing in Vietnam. The rockets flame toward the rich green garden, burst white hot and outward. It has been our curse to murder by proxy in this war, paying the hireling—vicarious execution. But for a moment in this film, we sit looking out the pilot's picture window on the world to be destroyed. Again and again, the missiles go out into forests and foliage and farms. And they appear to originate from where we sit. We would think from our very hearts.

That someone could even shoot this dispassionate record—a training film of history and the power of death—is for me a source of bleak amazement. And then to release it publicly, almost in naivete or demonic innocence—without ever seeing what it shows—that is a further symptom of hardened hearts. From whence does it come? This is the deadness of the machine of which we have spoken, the corruption of technology on hardware.

So many of the ironies strike cruel. But the most crushing comes from these closing lines of the letter (165–74) where the ones spatially closest to the blood of children do not feel it in the call and the course of their own. The hope is that behind the thin flat image in breast pockets, might be love for their own children. And that Great Buddha has said, might be enough to begin. The hope is that one as distant as bitter cold snow-fall from fevers and fires might remember to be so close.

An End to Words: No and Yes

In sum, it comes down to this—if the letter has journeyed toward us, there is a choice to be made in saying amen. And if the history of word and flesh is in us, then a simple No and Yes can carry us very far.

Epic Aside: "Vietnamese Letter"

By Daniel Berrigan

Part 1.

Dear friends, your faces are a constriction of grief in the throat
your words weigh us like chains, your tears and blood
fall on our faces. Prison; Vietnam, prison; U.S.
prison is our fate, mothers bear in prison,
(5)   our tongues taste its gall, bars spring up
from dragons' teeth, a paling, impaling us.
A universal malevolent will, crouched like a demon
blows winter upon us, stiffens our limbs in death, the limbs of women
(10)   and children.
Here, they hawk death in the streets, death in the hamburg joint
death in the hardware, death in the cobbler's hammer
death in the jeweler's glass, the classy showrooms of death.
Death, shouts the newsboy; death, oranges and lemons,
(15)   death in a candy wrapper.
Death, the cinema blares it; death!
And beyond it all, out of sight and mind
like an aquarium at midnight, a terminal hospital
like the eyes of a captive tiger
(20)   a colony of golden eyes
of bees in their cells, the miser's mine of jewels
throttling the moon underground–
you and I
our eyes like grapes under the nailed boots
(25)   our "why" dragged in the dust, a flayed animal's entrail
our "how long?" long as the lifeline thrown from God to Job.

Part 2.
If I were free! the phrase flies form our minds
        like a two-edged sword, an apocalypse cutting us free.
If we were free!
(30)   I would be your angel of deliverance

all my friends! between you and me the evening star arises,
>the jewel of
Buddha
>that compassionate mind encompasses the heavens!
(35) between those hands, their flower like
>>texture and repose
nothing, nothing is lost!
>>the tears of mothers sting like scorpions
the scorpion's sting falls like a tear.
(40) The universal order, fragile as eggshell, broken by the hammers
of mad bombers, heals
>>heals under that starry breath!
Lord Buddha, Lord Christ
>>whose hegemony, time and this world
is a compassionate unending search
(45) east and west, sunrise, sunset,
>for the least and lowliest, the wounded, the violated-
>>they live in us, the lords and servants of time
we live in them, lords and servants of time.

(50) And we shall break our chains like chains of sand
>>the conniving dissolute
puppets, their power
>>slumps like a rotten sawdust
their marauding hearts
(55) burst in a suppuration!
our mothers' tears, the Buddha's tears and Christ's
>>anoint us like a chrism
the sweet earth, punished by ruffians' fists
>>heals like a rising loaf, a bread of heroes
(60) and we shall sit and eat, the poor shall gather
>>under those bells and tears
from graves, ditches, huts, camps and caves
>>from the ends of the earth, from air and sea
the wretched, the maimed, the blind, the halt
(65) the dead, lively, restrung, joyous as grasshoppers—Buddha
>>and Christ,

Lord and servants of creation
    multiply that loaf in lotus fingers
the lost of existence
(70)   our immortal joy, flesh and family and tribe and nation
all things made new!

Part 3.
In that day the ingathering, but first the scattering
    in that day the banquet, but first the starvation
In that day the freedom, but first the prison
(75)   in that day the healing, but first the torture
In that day the music, but first the mourning
    in that day the justice, but first the false judgement
In that day the rebirth, but first the bloodletting.

Part 4.
    We must remember, great Buddha said, the place, the person, the
(80) time, when we first sat at table together. And the first generation
remembered.

    The second generation forgot the time. But they remembered the
house, and their brothers' and sisters' faces. And great Buddha said,
it is enough.

(85)   The third generation forgot the hour and the house. But they
sat with their brothers and sisters, here or there, now or then. And
great Buddha said, it is enough.

    The fourth generation forgot the hour, the house, and the faces of
their brothers and sisters. And great Buddha wept.

(90)   In the fifth generation, everyone was stranger. Men and women
were violated and tortured and outlawed. And great Buddha perished.
He died, a nameless peasant, in the general conflagration. He was buried
in a common grave. And the earth was void.

Part 5.
(100) If the birth of a child
    is sufficient reason
    to trim the lamps
    of the universe, to grace

seasons in a wedding garment,
(105) to wreathe in smiles
our stiff jointed discontent–
then it must be insisted
with equally rigorous logic;
the murder of a child is sufficient reason
(110) to burn like trash or offal
those hunting licenses
that go by the civilized
euphemism, "draft files," to endure
imprisonment, loss of repute
(115) the stigma of Cain
branded by the perfumed hands
of judges, politicos and church men
on the forehead of Abel.

In a time of sanctioned
(120) insanity, sane conduct
is an indictable crime.
In a time of omnicompetent
violence, compassion
is officially intolerable.
(125) In a time that celebrates
the apotheosis of Mars
Christ will languish
on ice for the duration.

Let us liberate reflection
(130) that many branched verdant tree
from its plague of befouling apes–
abstraction, inflation,
mock heroism, mock victimhood.

We;
(135) fed, clothed, housed
solicitously as the last
handful of survivors

of an endangered species.

It is hard in America, hard
(140) even in American prison
to take death seriously
Not hard for you, dear friends.
Official solicitude
evaporates with the distance.
(145) For chairman Caesar or Christ,
the messianic legions
kill with an equal fervor.
In either case, you are honored
though ignorant of your honor;—

(150) our superior motivation—
Pax Americana,
your bones to make our bread.

A. J. Muste: "we need a foreign
(155) policy for the children." Exactly
Thus;

The death of one child
brings down the universe
It is honorable to nurture
(160) even in prison, that endangered
flame, to mingle if so required
one's unwavering purpose
like an eagle's with that
bereft nest fallen life.

(165) Foreign, domestic policies, idem.
I.e., the nearest child is the furthest.
The nearest of blood is not
thereby most dear.
American airmen dumping
(170) their liquid fire upon faraway

hamlets, bear in breast pocket
Kodak prints of their children
Thus far corruption on high
of the call and course of the blood.

(175)   It is snowing tonight as I vigil. The first white fall of winter
bitterly cold. I think on
the fevers and horrors of Con Son.

No their No. YES to all else.

—— Chapter 7 ——

Prophet: Reading a Book Serious
in Life and Death

Prophecy is the voice that God gives to the silent agony, a voice
to the plundered poor, to the profaned riches of the world. It is a
form of living, a crossing point . . . God is raging in the prophet's
word.[1]—Abraham Heschel

IN 1972 I WAS a student at Union Seminary in New York City.[2] The anti-
war and civil rights movements had already left their form on my young
politics. I was to be sure a seminarian, but expected to emerge some sort
of community organizer with "a theological perspective." Frankly, most of
what I then believed was little more than sociology.

I recall at the time a course in the passion of Christ from an eminent
scholar. We were treated, among other historically critical data, to the
latest in archaeological evidence for the method of crucifixion, how the
ankles would be turned and the nails driven, the excruciating mechanics of death. The accuracy was impeccable, but the passion was at a safe
remove: past tense and lukewarm.

As providence would have it (from my perspective like an intervention
of the Word) Dan Berrigan just then walked out of Danbury Prison, where
he had done time in consequence of the 1968 Catonsville action, and into
the upper west side academic fortress. With him came the scent of prison.
The smells of the charnel house, of napalm and tiger cage tortures, were also
in the wind. He stood before us and read the news with Jacques Ellul in one
hand and the Revelation of John in the other. Present tense afire.

---

1. Heschel, *The Prophets*, 5.

2. Wylie-Kellermann, "Taking the Book with Life and Death Seriousness," in Dear,
ed., *Apostle*.

Never had I met anyone who took The Book with such life and death seriousness. Who thought in its own idiom. Who read it from the inside out. Who expected to find therein the powers of this world demythologized and exposed, and who took recourse to the Scriptures in hopes of imagining the real world (Buber). Who thereby resisted the former and bet his life on the latter.

I got knocked off my horse. A tidy worldview crumbled. I do not exaggerate: I was struck nearly dumb and wandered the seminary for a time more than a little lost. Berrigan noticed and one day called my name down a long basement hallway. Would I come up for Irish coffee? By and by: did I pray? Or read the Bible for any reason but a paper assigned? Had I ever seen these books: Merton on the "Desert Fathers" or Dorothy Day on the long loneliness? What signposts in the landscape did I follow? I took up the questions, like signposts in the landscape, and made them my own.

I have seen him do this with others since, some virtually in the grip of despair or death. Don't die, he would say. Come along, we need you. Don't be a conscious integer in the empire's spiritual body count. He made it seem as if resurrection and discipleship were synonyms.

And lo and behold: among us at Union a community of faith and resistance coalesced at the edge of the fortress wall. Berrigan was to us as the angel to John in Revelation who hands on the little scroll with the admonition, "Take it and eat; it will be bitter to your stomach, but like honey in your mouth." In the fortress cafeteria where sippers and samplers might taste, where Scripture was easy on the tongue, he urged us to eat the book. Swallow it whole, let it rumble with history in your guts.

It strikes me that this is always the character and consequence of his own biblical scholarship. Moreover, it may be the very reason his gifts of biblical interpretation are sometimes unaccounted. With barely an exception (Abraham Heschel would be one), he was viewed askance or completely ignored by the eminents of Union and its environs. I note that even Michael True's excellent compendium of Dan's work, *Daniel Berrigan: Poetry, Prose, and Drama*, runs thin on this category of writing. There his book on the Psalms is represented, but bring on the commentaries and extended meditations on Isaiah, Daniel, or Jeremiah, the life and prayer of Jesus, or Paul in chains, or the Acts of the Apostles, the vision of John the Divine or his most recent book, *Minor Prophets, Major Themes*.[3]

---

3. D. Berrigan, *Minor Prophets*. I wrote an introduction to the book, but the manuscript from Dan was so disorganized that I inquired of his editor if Dan was doing okay. His copy

It may serve to consider this new one at some length, to glimpse, as it were, the Berrigan method. To begin with, the book has a context. Yet another war was in the air with its ever perfected mechanics of death: cruise missiles, fuel air bombs, laser-guided et ceteras. Their shadows cross the pages. Their victims cry out.

This is to say, the drumbeat of war is not merely contextual background noise, it is virtually the occasion of recourse. Who would have thought that meditating on Haggai or Zechariah during the Persian Gulf War could preserve one's moral sanity? Indeed prove the very act of sanity? That is Berrigan's claim.

Here is a commentary that ought to be required reading in Old Testament seminars, though one suspects in some it would need to be "snuck in the door." For one, it's more than a commentary in the conventional sense. It jumps the track of passionless objectivity and moves readily across time, deftly implicating our lives and history.

This is not to suggest that conventional scholarship is preempted. The academics are, in fact, attended to and given their due. Berrigan defers to them and lets them speak, setting off their quotations to shade in the background or a historical skyline, to provide a subtle insight, or even to serve an ironic foil that may typify ourselves, our culture-bound imaginations and judgements.

But then. The commentary cracks and breaks open the genre. More than a hermeneutic is commended: it partakes in the prophetic method.

Even the style betrays an intuitive act of mimicry. These reflections are laid out on the page almost in fragments, with breaks or breaths or seams between. We are reminded how the prophetic utterances are gathered up (by the prophets themselves or mayhap their disciples) and stitched together—by their best light and inspirations—into more or less coherent books. The scholars, in their turn, never tire of reversing the process, sifting and separating the isolated "pericopes," even rearranging material according to their own lights. In any event, the seams in the prophetic literature are there to be recognized. You can feel them in the fits and leaps of reading. And in between, in the gaps and the cracks there is—what? sighs too deep for words? a silent agony? the wrestling with God or doubt or death? the movement of history? All these and more.

---

to me is inscribed, "Bill—your kind intro softens the blow of my creeping senility."

In reflecting on their words, Berrigan echoes the rhythm of this biblical style. In these seamly breaks on the page, what? His own silence and tears, the lunge of empire, more and the same.

Minor Prophets has its own pre-history. One hears portions offered and refined in retreats where this or that prophet was commended for common consideration. One imagines passages circulated hand to hand in jail cells, where prisoners of conscience abide and take heart. Certain fragments were surely commended among those preparing for public witness at, let us guess, a faith and resistance gathering. These are reflections hammered out in common decision.

One hastens to recall the Plowshares movement (now flourishing some five decades) and wonders: was Micah 4 the breaking and entry point for this book? Was it the way in, the door opening for Berrigan upon the whole rag-tag crew of the minor prophets?

A small irony: the minors were almost exclusively word prophets, but this commentary is shot through with present-day deeds and symbolic actions—more after the fashion of Jeremiah's signs: crashing down the pots, donning the yoke of empire, burying the loincloth, or investing in the absurd real estate of return. The actions that Berrigan invokes—at Pentagon and nuclear installations, laboratories and bunkers, in the streets and on the road of return with the Salvadoran campesinos—are invariably to the point. Across the time, by grounded imagination and faith, the word and the deed, the text and community, illuminate one another.

Dan's work is stunning in its ability to evoke the humanity of the prophets. Why should that seem such a rarity? From one theological extreme their canonization sanctifies them beyond reach, or (another version of the same thing) renders them faceless and empty conduits for the Word. From another, more sophisticated, they are reduced to cultural ciphers, instruments of the social forces that engage in the literary production of texts. Here, however, they are granted life, summoned in all their humanity. The Word is their struggle with conscience, their burning tears, their prayer and choice. In that sense, their humanity provokes our own.

And a conversation begins. Having heard them in their full humanness (with all the foibles and confusions and blind spots and shortfalls entailed) Berrigan claims a freedom to disagree, to criticize, even to call these mentors to account before community and our God. Do they challenge our lives and our hearts? Yes. But if we're in this thing together, then let us push back.

Their sexism comes to mind, with Hosea a flaming exemplar. Has he reduced his wife Gomer to a theological metaphor? Berrigan names this nothing less than abuse, and turns things back on the prophet with a Book of Gomer giving the silent nobody a voice. Is Hosea thereby written off and out? By no means. But in his exposure we are all made the better.

Or take Obadiah. How, Berrigan goes so far as to ponder, did this small-minded, rancorous prophet full of vengeful bitterness even make it into the canon? He supplants Yahweh with Mars, and sits smugly in the book. And yet: his humanity is so like our own in this very regard, as are his confusions. "Let Obadiah remind us of a long and bitter history of bellicose folly."[4] Even then the prophet has flashes of insight: if he's wrong about God, his take on empire is clear seeing and lucid.

Herewith another astonishment: that the prophets should be so unanimous, so univocal, so collectively relentless in their complaint against empire and its manifold forms, near and far. Has Berrigan inflated or inflicted this on the texts, bringing along and imposing some politic of his own? Read the texts. They are uncompromising. Perhaps our amazement is evidence against us that the imperial spirit, near and far, has muted and suppressed these neglected voices too long from our hearing.

There is one thing that Berrigan does bring unapologetically to these conversations and reflections: the commitment to nonviolence. It functions like the plumbline of Amos. He holds it out to us, out to the prophets. Its line goes straight to the heart of earth, straight to the heart of Christ. Of course, beside it empires are crooked and top-heavy walls shown ready to collapse. But prophets too may be bent, even their ideas of God might suffer a twist.

Another way of saying this is that the Gospels are never far from the page. The One who is the fullness of humanity, a prophet mighty in deed, steps from the wings now and again—not so much to speak as to show his wounds, to look the prophets in the eye and love them.

Dan, of course, was not big on being labeled a prophet. He once enclosed an article about him and Phil, by Garry Wills from *The Baltimore Sun*, entitled "Modern Prophets?"[5] His scribbled comment was, "Best thing about the idiot headline is the ?"[6]

---

4. D. Berrigan, *Minor Prophets,* 168.
5. Wills, "Modern Prophets?"
6. Enclosed in a letter to the author, March 1978.

Echoing Dorothy Day's derision of being called a saint, William String-fellow used to inveigh against those who labeled Dan Berrigan a prophet (or a poet) in order to write him off, beyond the realm of ordinary people, ordinary responsibility, normative and human action. I suppose it is not unlike the tactic of confining the Word of God only to a sacred book—in order to banish it safely from our scene, as though it were not everywhere and always to be recognized in common history and our lives.

The fact of the matter is that Dan Berrigan *is* both a prophet and a poet. His biblical theology and interpretation verify both vocations once again. But let none of us thereby be off the hook of mere Christianity's demands, nor fear to recognize, and even partake of, the bittersweet Word of God wherever it may be found.

Prophetic Aside: "Covenant and Conquest"

"Don't do it!" blurted out my friend, a friend as well of Daniel Berrigan's. "Don't stir that old pot. It's been rehashed and written about. A book even. Let it rest." I knew what he meant and feel it as trepidation even now. Later my friend relented. And I overcame the qualms.

I refer to "The Speech," which in full follows this preface. It was addressed to the Association of Arab American University Graduates in October of 1973. The invitation came by way of Eqbal Ahmad, the Pakistani scholar and anti-war activist who supported resistance movements globally. He'd recently been a labeled a co-conspirator with Dan, charged in the Harrisburg indictment. Between the invitation and the speech, the October/Yom Kippur War, began. Daniel hesitated, as he tells, but kept the date. He spoke as the bullets flew and the bombs fell—as the death tolls mounted.

I include it here in its entirety because I consider it genuine prophetic utterance and commend it so, even in the most facile sense of prescience. He spoke long before Gaza was turned to rubble, and the occupied territories littered with hilltop settlements, walls and separatist roads, making waters inaccessible and groves uprooted. Camps have been filled and then leveled. The death toll constant. But here even moreso, prophetic in the biblical sense, calling all in view to account.

This speech touched off a storm of criticism and debate. Some one hundred articles were devoted to it. The booklet, aforementioned, was published, gathering some of them. Debates were held. Hate letters received in volume. Awards and invitations withdrawn. The prophet paid up. As others have as well.

I have in my files a manuscript, "The Deluge Revisited," marked with his changes, and noting above "given at Haaahvahd in May, I think." With further editing, it was incorporated whole cloth into the full chapter devoted in his autobiography, *To Dwell in Peace*. It recounts the speech and its aftermath.[7]

What he neglects to tell there is that in the wake of the controversy, he made a trip to Israel/Palestine, Lebanon, Egypt, and Cyprus, accompanied by Paul Mayer. They met with people from a wide spectrum of factions, authorities, and traditions. Recordings of these conversations were carefully packaged and mailed home, but never arrived. A great loss was accomplished by the powers in suppressing the book intended. Add to this his

---

7. Forest also devotes a thorough chapter to it in *Lion's Den*, 179–87.

sense of betrayal by Palestinian leaders who face-to-face pledged disavowal of terrorism only to strike within weeks, killing twenty-one children in west Galilee. Disabused of naivete.

I confess to wincing at least once. Does Berrigan claim too much for himself as being a Jew in relation to church and state? It's hardly a Christian supercessionist trope, but is it form of appropriation? I want to believe he can speak outraged love from within the Hebrew tradition. I note that a quarter of his written corpus are volumes on the Hebrew Bible—all astonishing. He wrote commentaries on twenty-three of its books, including every single one of the prophets. He got inside of them and they in him.

I asked a young rabbi and a Hebrew scholar whom I trust and work beside in local movements to read Dan's speech, totally new to them. One called it a masterpiece of writing, though both wondered if he implied: were Jews supposed to be a light to the nations and so expected to be better than other peoples? That would be problematic. But if so, it would stem from his love and hope for the tradition, inhabiting it, and yearning for its fruits. I am reminded of Stokely Carmichael, later Kwame Ture, asking cryptically, "Dr. King, why do we have to be more moral than white folks?"[8]

Others at the time put it conversely. Was Israel, for a hundred reasons, a special case, entitled to special treatment and assistance? Dan responded:

> No nation state is entitled today to anything more than skepticism. On the other hand, every people, considered just as people, is a very special case. Including Palestinians, stuck in camps where wanton murder must surely recall other camps, other deaths. In the case of the Israelis, there is no need to invoke the past in order to arrive at a very special feeling. Their present situation would bring tears to stonier hearts than mine. Israelis are entitled to more compassion with every day that passes. Their leadership on the other hand—religious, military or political—is entitled to ever more contempt. So are their American masters. We must, in short, help save the Israeli people, as well as the Palestinian remnant—by making it impossible for the present policies, benighted and ruinous as they are, to continue.[9]

I also put the speech to two friends, rabbis deeply respected and loved, who were around at the time, remember it viscerally, and even took a sideways brunt or were otherwise in the thick of its controversy. They too

---

8. Harding, "Foreword," to Thurman, *Disinherited*, xii.

9. Berrigan, *Dwell*, 289.

have paid a price. As anti-war allies and opponents of Israeli policy, they responded immediately, with passionate concerns and comments. I include some of them in the form of questions for you to consider as you read.

- Was this, as so often said, the wrong audience? The wrong place, the wrong time?

- Should he have consulted more of his friends prior, especially Jewish ones, to tender insight?

- Is naming that, "some six million southeast Asians had been maimed, bombed, displaced, tortured, imprisoned, killed," a deliberate affront to the holocaust or shared horror at the scale of violence?

- In charging Israel with a failure to create new forms of political and social life for her own citizens, does he dismiss the kibbutz and moshav agricultural communities?

- Is there analysis implied for the role of international capitalism granting empire a successful divide-and-conquer strategy?

- Do these remarks sufficiently acknowledge a people, traumatized first of all by 1,700 years of Christian oppression, by the holocaust it sponsored, and those who fled it being turned away by every Christian populated state in the world?

- One could add, does this address what we are learning about collective, historical trauma?

- Like the best of the prophetic tradition, is there room allowed here for the great IF, the possibility of turning and transformation, space created for the choice to avoid catastrophe?

Three months after the speech (he had yet to do the firsthand trip), Dan joined Hans Morgenthau (the noted political scientist known for his "political realism"[10]) in a televised discussion.[11] They pressed one another firmly, back and forth. Asked, were he to make it again, if he had learned anything that would change the speech, Dan replied

> I can think of nothing, essentially, that I would want to retract, but
> I would want to add something: I don't think I conveyed my sense

10. Personal note: I read Morgenthau's *Politics of Nations* as a text in college. His theological counterpart was the "Christian realism" of Reinhold Niebuhr, who was his friend.

11. Berrigan and Morgenthau, *Great Berrigan Debate*, 25.

of love for Israel and for the Jewish people, which is very deep. I did say at one point that my speech was an act of love, of outraged love, but I should have developed that more. And I should have spoken more about my admiration for the social achievements and the agricultural and industrial achievements of Israel, especially in those early years when it was so difficult.[12]

Morgenthau's final remark, once acknowledging that Dan was irritating, wrong on a lot of points, but worth listening to, is a gracious one: "My personal respect for Father Berrigan has not been diminished at all. Perhaps my evaluation of his political wisdom has been somewhat impaired."

The Speech: Covenant and Conquest

Daniel Berrigan

Address to Association of Arab-American University Graduates, Washington, DC

October 19, 1973[13]

I come before you this evening, a non-expert in every field of human expertise, including the subject you have invited me to explore. I wish to include also in my field of inexpertise my own religious tradition: I am a non-expert Christian, by any conceivable standard. This admission is in the interest of both clarity of mind and of moral conduct. I am interested, as a Christian, in one thing; in so simple a thing as sane conduct in the world. The experts in my tradition, the theologians, the biblical scholars, and by and large, the hierarchy, go in another direction than mine. "Sane conduct" (whatever that means) is taken for granted; what really counts, is the jot and tittle of the tradition, or its worldly prospering, or its honorable reception among peoples. Sane conduct is taken for granted; are not Christians by definition sane, in touch with the truth, destined to share infallibly in their reward?

I say no. The exemplary conduct of expert Christians, as indeed of most experts in human disciplines, is to fiddle while the world burns. Hardly sane a kind of lethal fatalism looks equally upon combustible human

---

12. https://progressive.org/magazine/daniel-berrigan-moral-dilemma-middle-east-1974/.

13. Transcribed from a manuscript copy in my files.

flesh, shrugs its shoulders the better to nestle the violin, to coax from its entrails the immortal (and irrelevant) stroke . . .

Sane conduct in the world. Let me explain. I do not believe it is the destiny of human flesh to burn; and for that I am in trouble; as are my brother and my friends, to this day. I do not believe that a violin concerto, however immortal in execution, is the proper comfort to offer a napalmed child. I believe that the fiddler should come down from the roof, put his violin aside, take up an extinguisher, raise a cry of alarm, break down the intervening door. I believe that he should on occasion of crisis destroy property in favor of human life. I believe it is never allowed to destroy human life in order to save or preserve or enhance property. You see, I am a heretic in a consuming and killing culture, as well as in a complicit church.

These are troublesome statements; but do not call them naive, or shrug them off as generally accepted by the civilized; or, in the presence of scholars, as irrelevant.

Do not say, it is of course the generals who light fires; we deplore that. I answer; most scholars, most priests, most Jews, most Arabs, while they would prefer some less horrendous sight than the burning flesh of children, are not seriously shaken in their style of mind, their taxpaying, their consumerism, their spiritual, economic, or political complicity, by such "incidents."

I begin in so odious a way because I do not wish to narrow our question so sharply as to exclude ourselves from its orbit. I do not wish to take us off the hook, even while I wish to say something unequivocal about one instance of cruelty, racism, murder, as political tools.

It is of course scarcely possible to open the moral question of Israeli or Arab conduct today, without exciting the most lively passion, and risking the most serious charges. A war is underway. We are assured by the Israelis, and by most of the Jewish community throughout the world, that the war is a war of survival. We are assured just as vehemently by the Arabs that the war is one of expansion and aggression by Israel . . . formerly the Jews strike the first blow, now it is the Syrians. Always violence, always more violence . . . Moreover, the interests of the super powers are deeply imbedded in near eastern soil. Those interests include western oil contracts, and east and west, an impalpable element of outreach, something hard to define, a cold war afflatus perhaps, something called "ideological spheres of influence." In any case, both east and west are shoring up their interests with that most concrete and bloody proof of devotion; arms, and more arms.

In all this welter and fury, are there any signs of help? Let us point to one most important one. A cease fire has been offered by Egypt; something unprecedented in the history of this conflict. Moreover, the terms of the cease fire seem reasonable and free of Arab arms-rattling. The offering includes a declaration of de facto respect for the existence of Israel, a de facto state; it asks for a return to the boundary lines drawn before the six day war in 1967. It asks negotiation on the fate of Palestinian refugees. The seriousness and sanity of the cease fire offer, therefore, I believe is helping set the stage for a fruitful alternative. In supporting the Egyptian proposal, I hope to answer those who would make the present war into an Israeli spasm of survival. Nothing of the sort. Or those would make the critics of this war, into proponents of Israeli extinction. Nothing of the kind. Or those who would make critics of the United States, into supporters of the Soviet Union; nothing of the sort.

In calling attention to the Egyptian proposal, I am simply urging that attention be paid to the first sane option which has arisen in the course of this suicidal adventure. Indeed, there are no "sides" worth taking: there are immense numbers of peoples whose lives and rights are being violated, degraded, denied. Any real solution will take into account these people; people without country, people endangered, people invaded.

How carefully one must proceed in these matters, if he is not to worsen an already tortured situation: I endorse the Egyptian cease fire proposal; but I abominate many aspects of the Egyptian regime, of the sheikdoms, of Jordan, of Syria; their capacity for deception is remarkable, even for our world. Their contempt for their poor could be called legendary, were it not also horrifyingly modern. Their willingness to oil the war machinery of the super powers makes them accomplices of western war criminals. Their cupidity is matched only by their monumental indifference to the facts of their world—which, as their conduct insures, remains a stagnant third world. No, I offer no apologia tonight for the Arab states, any more than for Israel.

I will not begin by "taking sides"; nor indeed will I end by "taking sides." I am sick of "sides"; which is to say, I am sick of war; of wars hot and cold; of all their metaphors and deceits and ideological ruses. I am sick of the betrayal of the mind and the failure of compassion and the neglect of the poor. I am sick of Secretaries of State and their works and pomps (and peace prizes). I am sick of torture and secret police and the apparatus of fascists and the rhetoric of leftists. Like Lazarus staggering from his grave, or the ghost of Trotsky I can only groan; "We have had enough of that; we have been through all that."

When I received an invitation to address you some months ago, I winced. Another crisis? If the nerve ends of Israelis and Arabs were raw, so were mine . . . More; why should I enter your yard on a cleanup project when my own, American, was a moral shantytown? . . . And the war broke, and I winced again; and very nearly begged off. Then a better, second thought occurred; something like this. If it was important to speak up while a nonwar, at least an absence of war held—then why not when a war broke? Indeed, did not the need for dispassion and reason and courage increase, while the guns were cutting down whatever sanity remained? If the first casualty of war was the truth, might it not be important to prevent, at least on one scene, that mortal casualty from occurring?

It is in this spirit I hope to proceed. As a Westerner and a Christian, I believe it is my duty to explore with you certain neglected aspects of this war. I do not wish to heap conflict upon conflict. If I seem to concentrate upon the conduct of Israel, it is for reasons which to me at least, are profound, of long pondering and finally inescapable. It is not merely because my government, which has brought endless suffering to the world, is supporting Israel. It is not merely because Americans as well as Israelis, have in the main given their acquiescence to the Nixon ethos. The reasons go deeper, and strike harder; they are lodged in my soul, in my conception of faith and transcendence, in the vision Jews have taught me of human conduct. (To put the matter as simply as I know how) I am paying an old debt. It is a debt of love; more properly, a debt of outraged love. I am a western Christian, in resistance against my government and my church. That position, as I read it, makes me something very like a Jew. It is of the uneasy circle, in which I dwell ever widening, contracting, including, excluding, that I wish to speak. I am a Catholic priest, in resistance against Rome. I am a Jew, in resistance against Israel. But let me explain. A common assumption exists in the West, buttressed by massive historical and religious argument, to the effect that Israel is exempt from moral criticism. Her people have passed through the gentile furnace; how then shall the goy judge the suffering servant? And is not the holocaust the definitive argument for the righteousness of this people, heroically determined to begin again, in a promised land, that experiment in survival which so nearly went awry, so often, under such constant assault at our hands?

In such a way, bad history is mightily reinforced by bad faith. The persecutor is a poor critic. His history weighs on him; like a bad parent, he alternates between cruelty and indulgence, without ever striking the mean of love.

In such a way, Christians yield to Israel the right to her myths; to indulge them, to enlarge them, to live by them, even to call them biblical truths. If the Jews are indeed the people of promise, and Israel the land of promise; then it must follow that God has willed the two to coincide. The means? They are swallowed up in the end, they disappear into glory. And if the means include domestic repression, deception, cruelty, militarism? And if the classic refugee people is creating huge numbers of refugees? And if technological warfare has become the instrument of expansion, and preemptive warfare the instrument of so-called peace? And if this people, so proud, so endowed with intelligence and artistry, so purified by suffering, sends its military missionaries into parts of the world where the people are bleeding under the heel of jackboots? (Israeli military advisors in Iran, Israeli military advisors in Ethiopia.) And if these advisors (that cruel euphemism under whose guise America kindled the Vietnam holocaust) and if these advisors are sought and hired because Israelis have become as skilled in the fashioning of espionage and violence as ever were their oppressors? Are such means as these swallowed in glory? Or do they stick in the throat of those who believe, as Judaism taught the world to believe; "Thou shalt not kill"?

I started to say something about my own church, and I proceed to talk about Israel. I do so advisedly. I do so because today my church has helped Israel exegete her own texts—wrongly, harmfully, as I believe. My church has helped Israel in that project which is almost invariably the project of the settler state—whether of South Africa or Israel or the United States—which is to seek a biblical justification for injustices against humanity.

For a Christian who is trying to understand and live by his own tradition, this confusion of Bible and imperialism represents an altogether unique tragedy. We in the USA learned to bear the filthy weight of South African religious violence, even while we abominated it. We learned to survive the filthy weight of American religious violence, even while we abominated it. In both cases, we tried to separate the corrupt cultural elements from the truth of a tradition, and to live by the latter. We learned to do this, because we knew at least something of the history of Christianity, in both its criminal and saintly aspects. But you must understand our horror, our

91

impoverishment, almost our sense of amputation. For while we had known criminal Christian communities, and suffered at the hand of our own renegades, and seen Vietnam assaulted in the name of Christian civilization—we had never known a criminal Jewish community.

We had known Jewish communities that were a light to the gentiles, that were persecuted, all but erased, that remained merciful, eloquent, prophetic. But something new was occurring before our eyes . . . The Jews arose from the holocaust, a cause of universal joy; but the Jews arose like warriors, armed to the teeth. They took possession of a land, they exiled and destroyed old Arab communities, they (a minority) imposed the harshest minority laws on those who were once the majority of citizens. Then, they flexed their muscles; like the goyim, the idolaters, the "inhabitants of this earth," like Babylon and Egypt and Assyria; like those kingdoms which Israel's own prophets summoned to judgment, Israel entered the imperial adventure. She took up the imperial weapons, she spread abroad the imperial deceptions.

In the space of 25 years, this metamorphosis took place. The wandering Jew became the settler Jew; the settler ethos became the imperial adventure. More, the thought of Nietzsche, of Camus and Fanon was vindicated; the slave became master, and created slaves. The slave master created a "shadowy other." Israel had emerged from the historical shadows determined to take her place in the company of nations: an ambition no decent conscience could object to. But the price of her emergence was bitter and heavy; and it continues. That price indeed, neither Israel nor ourselves have yet counted up. But we do know a few of the human items who have been placed on the block of Israeli hegemony. They include some one and a half million refugees, whom Israel has created in the process of creating herself.

And let us not hesitate to start the price in Israeli coinage. Something like this: not only a dismal fate for foreign and indigenous victims, but the failure to create new forms of political and social life for her own citizens. The coinage of Israel is stamped with the imperial faces whose favor she has courted; the creation of an elite of millionaires, generals and entrepreneurs. And the price is being paid by Israel's so-called oriental Jews, the poor, the excluded, the prisoners and the Palestinians. Do we seek analogies for this "sublime adventure of return"? They are not hard to come by. But they do not exist, alas, in the dreams of Zionist rhetoricians; they exist rather in the real world, where Zionist violence and repression joins the violence and repression of the great (and little) powers; a common method, a common dead end.

It is entirely logical for instance, that Russia, which crushed the Czechs, is now in process of crushing the Ukranians, and bottling the brains of political dissidents on the shelves of psychiatric morgues. It is entirely logical that the US, which determined to crush the Vietnamese, also spent a considerable part of the '60s "mopping up" political dissidents at home. Imperialism has no favorites; it freezes all it touches. It is thus not to be wondered at that torture has been applied to Israeli citizens as well as to suspect Palestinian terrorists. It is logical that Israeli workers are exploited, even while indigenous peasants are rooted out and their villages destroyed. It is logical that housing for the poor is rarer and rarer, even while housing for the affluent refugees stands empty. Logical too, that racist ideology, which brought the destruction of the Jewish communities at the hands of the Nazis, should now be employed by the state of Israel, fostering the myth of the "barbarian Arab," and of Israel the "sublime expression of the liberation of the Jewish people."

If only a people could know itself! If only a people could stand back from the welter of claim, the barrage of propaganda, the blood myths of divine election, the rhetoric which assures it that its case before history is unique and virtuous and in fact, unassailable. If such could happen, Israel would see, and indeed some of her own resisters, some of her own victims, some of her own friends, do see; that she is rapidly evolving into the image of her ancient adversaries. Her historic adventure, which gave her the unassailable right to "judge the nations," has veered off into an imperial misadventure; she carries in the world, the stigmata of the settler nation; she is ranged not at the side of those she once stood with, and succored and protected from extinction; the poor, the despised, the victims of the powers of this world. No. She has closed books, her sacred books. Her prophets shed no light upon her politics. Or more to the point, she has not passed from a dispossessed people to a democratic state, as she would claim, she has passed from a dispossessed people to an imperial entity.

And this (I say with a sinking heart) is to the loss of all the world; to her own loss, and to the loss of Palestinians, and Americans, and Jews in the diaspora, and Jews in Russia, and the Pope in the Vatican, and Vietnamese, and Cambodians, and South Africans, and Chileans. For it is of the moment to us all (I almost said of the supreme moment) that Jews retain their own soul, their own books, their own vivid sense of alternate paths to the light, so that Jews might be the arbiter and advocate of the downtrodden of the earth. On the scales of the spirit, as nations are finally judged, it is a tragedy beyond calculating that the State of Israel should become the repository and finally the tomb, of the Jewish soul. That in place of Jewish passion for the poor and forgotten, Israel should legislate evictions, uprootings, destruction of goods, imprisonment, terrorism. That in place of Jewish peaceableness, Israel should legislate a law of expanding violence. That in place of Jewish prophetic wisdom, Israel should launch an Orwellian nightmare of double talk, racism, fifth-rate sociological jargon, aimed at proving its racial superiority to the people it has crushed . . .

My sense of loss here is something more than academic. Let me say this: when an American is resisting the murder of the Vietnamese people, one of his chief sources of strength is the conviction that around the world, there exists a spiritual network of those who have put their lives to the same resistance. A network of conscience. One is joined in this way, to Blacks and Cubans and Brazilians and Chileans and so many others, who have made it their life's work to create a better method than murder for dealing with human conflicts.

Now at any moment of my struggle, in the underground or in prison, did resisters such as I take comfort from the conduct of the State of Israel? Could we believe the rhetoric that she was packaging and huckstering into the world? I must answer no, in the name of all. Rather than being comforted, I was tempered and sobered. Indeed I knew that I must take into account two bitter facts about Israel: 1) that if I were a conscientious Jew in Israel I would have to live as I was living in America; that is, in resistance to the state. And 2) the reaction of Israel to my conscience would be exactly the reaction of the United States; that is to say, I would either be hunted by the police, or in prison.

Which brings me to a reflection nearer home; the American Jewish community and the Vietnam war.

By and large, that community's leaders, fervent in support of Israel, were also fervent in support of Nixon. A massive support indeed; and it did not gather in a political vacuum. Nixon, a political manipulator of great astuteness, knew that religious interests were a fulcrum on world events. So he was able to mute the horrific facts of the Vietnam War in light of Jewish concern for the well-being of Israel. The plain fact was that Ms. Maier wanted Phantom jets and Nixon wanted re-election. Another fact was also plain, if of less moment to either party; in Nixon's first term alone, some six million southeast Asians had been maimed, bombed, displaced, tortured, imprisoned, killed. This was one of those peculiar facts which must be called free floating; for many, it was a statistic, it did not signify. To put the matter brutally, the American Jewish leaders were capable of ignoring the Asian holocaust, in favor of economic and military aid to Israel.

Those of us who resisted the war, had to live with that fact. The fate of the Vietnamese was as unimportant as the Zionist leadership in our midst, as was the fate of Palestinians.

And if there is an element of hope in all this, one must of course pay tribute to that great majority of the American Jewish community, which in fact refused the bait offered by Nixon. Their acute and legitimate concern for Israel never became a weapon against Vietnamese survival. They refused that immoral choice, offered them so enticingly by a leadership which would make the price of one people, the extinction of another. They rejected that choice, and for that, we honor them . . .

I cannot but reflect how strong is the irony of this occasion; a Jesuit priest speaking of such things. A member of the classic oppressor church calls to account the historic victims of Christian persecution; an irony indeed!

With what reluctance I must speak then, conscious as I am of the crimes of my church against the Jewish people! At the same time, I cannot consent that the crimes of the fathers purchase my silence in fact of the crimes of Israel. Indeed, the irony of the occasion goes deeper than I can easily say. History has spun us about, a game of blind man's bluff. In America, in my church, I am a kind of a Jew. I am scarcely granted a place to teach, a place to worship, a place to announce the truths I live by. I stand in front of St. Patrick's Cathedral to pray for the victims of our ceaseless rage, I stand in front of the White House. And a question arises from both powers; how shall we deal with this troublesome Jew?

How does a Jesuit, a member of the church elite, come to such trouble? How does the son of the oppressor come to be oppressed? Even while the oppressed, the Zionist, the state of Israel, becomes the oppressor? I can offer only the clumsiest of clues. The power of the Jew, as indeed the power of the priest, arises from the questions which his life raises. It comes from no other source. It cannot come from adherence to the power of this world. When the priest becomes the civil servant of the Papal State, he loses his true dignity, he comes a secular nonentity. His passion for justice is blunted, his sense of the sufferings of the world grows dim and abstract. And the same holds for the Arab as for the Jew. Human life today is meant to raise a cry against legitimated murder. Our lives are meant to be a question mark before humanity, but a Zionist or a Vatican Catholic or an Arab apologist erases that momentous dignity. He becomes a zero, his soul is torn in two. Let Amos Kenan, the Israeli writer, speak the bitter truth; for all such betrayals of the human vocation. "I believe that Zionism came to establish a shelter for persecuted people, and not to persecute other people. Even when the facts strike me in the face and prove to me ex post facto that Zionism was nothing but a useful tool to deprive the Palestinian Arab people of their homeland, I will stick to the lie."

Let him stick to the lie. But let him also know, the lie sticks to him. It sticks in the throat, it sticks to the very soul. To the point where a Christian must continue to ask of Israel those questions which Israel proscribes, ignores, fears. Where indeed are your men of Wisdom? Where are your peacemakers? Where are your prophets? Who among you speaks the truth to power? Where are the voices that abhor militarism, torture, bombing, degrading alliances with the great powers?

Israel knows the answer. She has dealt with "this people," who are her truest people. Her peacemakers, her men, of truth and wisdom, are dispensed with, are disposed of. They have neither power nor voice in the affairs of the Israeli state. Many of them are in prison, or hounded from the scene, living in exile. They are equivalent Palestinians, no voice, trampled rights non-persons.

These are among the most sorrowful facts of the world we must live in. Israel, that millennial dream, belonged not only to Jews, but to all of mankind—it belonged to me. But the dream has become a nightmare. Israel has not abolished poverty and misery, rather she manufactures human waste, the by-products of her entrepreneurs, her military industrial complex. Israel has not written justice into law; she has turned the law of nature to a mockery, creating ghettoes, disenfranchised peoples, exiles, hopeless minorities, cheap labor forces, Palestinian migrant workers. Israel has not freed the captives; she has expanded the prison system, perfected her espionage, exported on the world market that expensive blood ridden commodity, the savage triumph of the technologized West; violence and the tools of violence. Her best citizens, who would in a free society, be free to dissent, free to advocate change, free to denounce crime, are silenced. In Israel, military might is increasingly both the method and the goal of political existence. Her absurd generals, her military junk, are paraded on national holidays before the narcoticized public. The model is not the kingdom of peace, it is an Orwellian transplant, taken bodily from Big Brother's bloody heart. In Israel, the democratic formula is twisted out of all recognition; the citizens exist for the well-being of the state. It follows, as the imperialist corollary, that that measure of terrorism and violence and murder is applied to dissidents, as shall guarantee the "well-being of the state," as the ominous phrase is peddled by those in power.

And all the while, an astonishing spate of rhetoric assures the world that Israel is a "sublime expression of the Jewish people's liberation," that the state embodies the good of "this people." It is necessary to state, with all the vigor possible to outraged truth and love, it is, not by the sedulous Salesmen who come to the Washington Blight House, yamulka in hand, dockering for a larger part in our "definitive solution" to the world's divisions—it is not by such that we will be redeemed.

Who will save us from such saviors? I venture to say; neither Egypt nor Libya nor Syria nor Al Fatah nor Golda Maier nor General Dayan; neither Migs nor Phantom jets nor nuclear skills. After such saviors do the gentiles lust.

The present course, I suggest, leads to one dead end for both sides. The settler state and the long settled state, both are in process of metamorphosing into slave states, clients of the fascist super powers. At home, a slave mentality is progressively created, the reduction of rights of citizens, slave labor forces, slave wages, the domination of slave masters, politicized police, the militarization of national goals and policies.

Then the same process is internationalized. Such a nation inevitably becomes the instrument of great power politics. It serves as a foreign military base for one of another of the world powers; to that purpose everything is mobilized, including the truth itself.

My concluding word is addressed especially to the Arab peoples. My critique of you is ultimately my critique of Israel. Both of you have ignored your historical symbols. But in different ways. Israel has betrayed her exodus, by turning it into a military conquest. And you have responded in kind, equally blind, equally vain. And what else could you do? . . . Eqbal Ahmad, one of your most creative minds, has suggested a massive, worldwide "reversal of symbols." What if the Arab peoples throughout the world, were to raise a great cry, after the manner of Gandhi, Martin King, Chavez? What if your cry became, "Let my people go?" What if your peoples were on the roads of the world, knocking at the doors of the embassies of Russians,

Americans, Israelis, demanding a cease fire, demanding repatriation; and at the same time, taking into account the fears of the Jewish community, welcoming her peoples to your side, breaking the iron circle which condemns both sides Israelis and Arabs alike to death dealing and to death?

— Chapter 8 —

Orderly of Nonviolence: With Camus
in the House of the Dying

This was the time of the flu epidemic and the wards were filled and the halls too. Many of the nurses became ill and we were very short-handed. Every night before going off duty there were bodies to be wrapped in sheets and wheeled away to the morgue. When we came on duty in the morning, the night nurse was performing the same grim task . . . Nursing was like newspaper work. It was impossible to suffer long over the tragedies which took place every day. One was too close to them to have perspective. They happened too continuously. They weighed on you, gave you a still and subdued feeling, but the very fact that you were continually busy left you no time to brood . . . One thing I was sure of, and that was that these fellow workers and I were performing an act of worship.—Dorothy Day, *The Long Loneliness*[1]

IN THE COVID SPRING of 2020,[2] when I told my friend John that I was re-reading Camus's *The Plague*, he responded, "It was Camus and *The Plague* which sent me to jail and helped get me through it. Plagues may come and go (you never know) and the key is not just the initial response but to continue with steadfast commitment." He did three years for refusing induction during the American war in Vietnam. I knew exactly what he meant.

No coincidence, in the seventies, Daniel Berrigan had commended the novel to us as a group of New York seminarians then in his tutelage. Berrigan read Camus in French. His own seminary training with the Jesuits had included a final year in France. While he was there, the French were

1. Day, *Long Loneliness*, 91–92.
2. Parts of this chapter were published as Wylie-Kellermann, "Review of *The Plague*."

defeated in Vietnam after the siege of Dien Bien Phu. I wonder if it was that very year he himself read *Le Peste*.[3]

The story takes place in the city of Oran, a French Algerian town on the Mediterranean coast, sometime in the 1940s. For ten months the city suffers an epidemic of bubonic plague and is subsequently locked down with gates shut and guarded. The novel is indeed a mine of parallels and insights relevant to our own experience in the dangerous days of pandemic.

The first victim of the plague in Oran is the concierge at the apartment building where resides Dr. Reiux, the novel's main character. As if to mimic, among the first victims of COVID-19 in New York was a much beloved Bronx doorman, Juan Sanabria, memorialized in *The New Yorker* magazine.[4]

For far too long in Oran, even as the deaths mount, denial is the official order of the day. Dr. Rieux, who only at the conclusion will acknowledge being our narrator, is the first to discern the situation. He repeatedly presses town officials to face facts and act quickly, but they are loathe to acknowledge the reality lest appearing alarmist; they equivocate, mince words, wish to wait and see, defer to other authority, or publish discreet decrees in obscure places. Rieux persuades them to convene the health committee.

> Dr. Richard hesitated, then fixed his eyes on Rieux.
>
> "Please answer me quite frankly, Are you absolutely sure it's plague?"
>
> "You're stating the problem wrongly. It's not a question of the term I use; it's a question of time."[5]

Once the gates are shut, a sense of being exiled in one's own home settles upon the residents—"that sensation of a void within, which never left us, that irrational longing to hark back to the past or else to speed up the march of time, and those keen shafts of memory that stung like fire."[6] The ache of separation is compounded when mail, a source of contagion, is halted and residents are left with cryptic ten-word telegrams to communicate with distant loved ones. The daily death toll and its curve becomes

---

3. Berrigan made several trips to France; one for his Jesuit Tertianship 1953–54, another for a sabbatical 1963–64; one for a visit with Thich Nhat Hanh and the Cannes film festival in 1972; and yet another of several months with Nhat Hanh outside Paris in 1974.

4. See Blitzer, "The Life and Death."

5. Camus, *Plague*, 50.

6. Camus, *Plague*, 71.

a constant and eventually deadening feature of the news. Schools are commandeered for emergency hospitals. Sports fields become isolation encampments. Funerals are accelerated with ceremonials reduced to the barest minimum or none at all. Mass gravesites are opened. And structural injustice, in its way, is exposed.

> Profiteers were taking a hand and purveying at enormous prices essential foodstuffs not available in the shops. The result was that poor families were in great straits, while the rich went short of practically nothing. Thus, whereas plague by its impartial ministrations should have promoted equality among the townsfolk, it now had the opposite effect and, thanks to habitual conflict of cupidities, exacerbated the sense of injustice rankling men's hearts.[7]

Searching such parallels, a contradiction arises. Under COVID-19, both cases and deaths are widely disproportionate in African American communities, exposing the realities of racial inequity. As "re-opening" the economy becomes a forced agenda, the violence to US Black and Brown communities begins to look genocidal. The population of historic Oran (where Camus lived for some time in the early forties) was at least half North African Arab (socially and politically oppressed) but how they might have fared under plague is not reflected in the novel's, by all appearances, "European" city. Camus was not unaware of the extreme injustices they faced (he had been forced out of the country in 1940 for writing against these, and his passionate articles on the topic were gathered in *Algerian Chronicles*, the last book published before his sudden death in 1960), but they remain absent here.

Still, it's worthy of note that when Berrigan travelled to South Africa from France in 1963, his talk revolved around the novel.

> My reflection dwelt on the theme of Camus's novel *The Plague* as a useful ruling metaphor for South Africa. In the novel, someone inquires of the doctor, the antihero of the story: Why did the epidemic strike the city? He replies, they forgot to be modest, that is all. I found the words disturbingly on the mark. The immodesty of the racist regime of South Africa was apparent. But the plague could by no means be isolated there, as a matter of either principle or fact. Who could dwell in America and be ignorant of a like pretension, pride of place, intransigent racism infecting us also?[8]

---

7. Camus, *Plague*, 237.
8. Berrigan, *Dwell*, 160–61.

For being atheist "existentialists," Camus and his doctor are competent and critical engagers of theology. Fa. Paneloux, a Jesuit priest and locally celebrated academic, preaches a sermon early in the plague's occupation. The Cathedral is full and his theme is set: "Calamity has come upon you, my brethren, and, my brethren, you deserved it." Erudite, biblically and historically literate, he proclaims, that God "has turned his face away" and "loosed on you this visitation." (Less erudite and literate versions of this theme may be heard in certain pulpits these days—often with big claims to knowing God's judgement and precise intent). "The just man," says Paneloux, "has nothing to fear, but the evildoer has good cause to tremble." His word of consolation is to seek the good that God is working through this plague, to repent, and to offer up a prayer of love.[9]

Paneloux does not thereby slip away and disappear from the story. He remains pastorally and physically present to the sick and dying. Eventually, he and Reiux vigil together at the bedside of a child afflicted. It is one of two deaths Camus describes for pages in excruciating detail. After a spasm passes, his "flesh wasted to the bone, the child lay flat, racked on the tumbled bed, in grotesque parody of crucifixion." As morning comes the boy wails again in agony, Paneloux sinks to his knees and cries out, "My God, spare this child!" But the wails flutter into silence and it's over. As they depart hastily, Rieux rounds angrily on the priest: "Ah! That child, anyhow, was innocent, and you know it as well as I do!"[10]

Pursuing him down the hall, Paneloux presses, "I understand. That sort of thing is revolting because it passes our human understanding. But perhaps we should love what we cannot understand." The doctor replies, "No, Father. I've a very different idea of love. And until my dying day I shall refuse to love a scheme of things in which children are put to torture."[11]

The child's death, however, shifts something in the priest. In response, he becomes more gently charitable, but also more absolute. One had to believe All or Nothing. And who could believe Nothing? When he himself takes sick, he acts this out by refusing to call the doctor and putting himself in God's hands alone. Though his symptoms are not typical of the plague, he dies. Rieux attends him in the end, and for the official log, lists him as a "Doubtful Case."[12]

9. Camus, *Plague*, 94, 95.

10. Camus, *Plague*, 215, 217, 218.

11. Camus, *Plague*, 218.

12. Camus, *Plague*, 234.

I've sometimes wondered if Berrigan was drawn to the book because the Jesuit is so directly addressed by Camus. Dan's own take on the priest character regarded him "as an example of religious absurdity . . ."

> Pere Paneloux, the "compleat Jesuit" of Oran in *The Plague*. He thinks that religion exists in order to "prove something." This has to do, in his case, with an apologetic of religion that will make of God the prime inquisitor of all; the great final judge between the righteous and the outsiders.[13]

In his recommendation of the novel to us, Dan made no mention of the priest, but only the ethic of the doctor who aspired to the simplest virtues of humanity and decency, which in this case meant "doing his job." Berrigan would shortly undertake similar support work with terminal cancer patients as an orderly at St. Rose's Hospice.[14]

I've only recently learned that Camus began plotting the novel during the Nazi occupation when he was taking a medical cure for tuberculosis in Le Panelier, a village in the south of France. It turned out to be adjacent to another town, Le Chambon, where Protestants Andre and Magda Trocme were then pastoring the entire village into a "sanctuary city," hiding and shepherding to safety, over the period of the war, more than 3,000 Jewish refugees. Its residents took risks, suffered loss, and some were killed—all as a matter of course, as though it were simply in the nature of things and part of what it meant to be human (see Philip Hallie's account in *Lest Innocent Blood Be Shed*).[15] Though already then himself a part of the French resistance, it is uncertain whether Camus knew these details. But then again if he knew them would he record them? His notebooks betrayed no evidence. However, by coincidence, the doctor's name in Le Chambon was Rioux.[16]

In 1948, the year after the book was published, Camus addressed Christians at a Dominican monastery. He had a complaint and a yearning. It seemed to him that as the preparations for war were undertaken, as the bloody toll of victims grew, as fear spread, the church remained unconscionably silent, or spoke only in an abstract and obtuse style. He, by turn, was candid and blunt:

13. D. Berrigan, *No Bars*, 137.

14. D. Berrigan, *We Die*.

15. Hallie, *Innocent Blood*.

16. Zaretsky, "Out of a Clear Blue Sky."

For a long time during those frightful years I waited for a great voice to speak up in [the Church], I, an unbeliever? Precisely. For I knew that the spirit would be lost if it did not utter a cry of condemnation when faced with force . . . What the world expects of Christians is that Christians should speak out, loud and clear, and that they should voice their condemnation in such a way that never a doubt, never a slightest doubt, could arise in the heart of the simplest person. That they should get away from abstraction and confront the blood-stained face history has taken on today. The grouping we need is a grouping of people resolved to speak out clearly and to pay up personally.[17]

When Berrigan reworked the transcript of the Catonsville trial into play form, he used a portion of this quotation among the voices of a moral chorus interspersed throughout.[18]

Though they rarely talk much, Rieux's main conversation partner is Jean Tarrou, a stranger visiting Oran who remains when its gates are locked. Not so parenthetically, *all* the conversations of this book are between men. At a time when Simone de Beauvoir was speaking and writing in French existentialist circles, this is an obvious contradiction. Rieux's mother, quiet and behind the scenes, is barely an exception.

Because Rieux acquires his journal, Tarrou becomes virtually a co-narrator of the book, a keen observer and second reliable witness. Almost casually, he offers to assist the doctor, organizing a squad of frontline volunteers, removing bodies and undertaking the sanitary works of mercy.

Once Tarrou accompanies the doctor on an evening visit to an asthma patient. When their host offers the two access to his apartment's rooftop view, Tarrou seizes the moment to tell at length his story. That accounting is a key to the book, in my view, though it covers only a dozen pages. I will try to render it in but a few paragraphs. The youthful crux of it involves a tale of attending court one day with his father. There Jean's young attention is completely taken with empathy for the defendant, perhaps guilty, but displaying all the quirky elements of being human. Suddenly, he realizes what his father, the prosecuting attorney in red robes, is doing. "[His] mouth spewed out long, turgid sentences like an endless stream of snakes. I realized he was clamoring for the prisoner's death, telling the jury that it owed it to society to find him guilty . . ." And he realizes further that over and over it had fallen to his father, "in the course of his

17. Camus, "The Unbeliever and the Christians," 71.
18. D. Berrigan, *Trial*, 56.

duties, to be present at what's politely termed the prisoner's last moments, but would better be called murder in its most despicable form."[19] For him, this marked a momentous change of heart and the eventual recognition that the whole social order around him was based upon death. Having dedicated his life to resisting such violence, but suffering compromise in the process, he now looks back:

> And thus, I came to understand that I, anyhow, had had the plague through all those long years in which, paradoxically enough, I'd believed with all my soul that I was fighting it. I learned that I had had an indirect hand in the deaths of thousands of people . . . So that is why I resolved to have no truck with anything which, directly or indirectly, for good reason or bad, brings death to anyone or justifies others' putting them to death . . . All I maintain is that there are pestilences and there are victims, and it's up to us, so far as possible, not to join forces with pestilences.[20]

It is certainly possible to join forces with a pandemic, by indifference, criminal ineptitude, or by institutional policy and outright design. We are witnesses. Yet, here we are officially on notice that the plague is more than plague. It does not cease to be an epidemic, but it is also metaphor, even parable. For what? Fascism? Occupation? War? Violence itself? Any and all, I suggest. And it represents a veritable commitment to nonviolence.

Tarrou tells Rieux that given pestilences and victims he tries to be at least an "innocent murderer," though he acknowledges a third and very rare category: true healers. "It must be a hard vocation. That is why I decided to take, in every predicament, the victim's side, so as to reduce the damage done."[21] Here in simplicity is an ethic.

In 1970, Berrigan wrote a "Letter to the Weathermen" that included like observations:

> When madness is the acceptable public state of mind, we're all in danger, all in danger; for madness is an infection in the air. And I submit that we all breathe the infection and that the movement has at times been sickened by it . . . A revolution is interesting insofar as it avoids the plague like the plague it promised to heal. Ultimately if we want to define the plague as death (a good definition), a pro-human movement will neither put people to death

---

19. Camus, *Plague*, 248.
20. Camus, *Plague*, 254.
21. Camus, *Plague*, 254.

nor fill the prisons nor inhibit freedoms nor brainwash nor torture enemies nor be mendacious nor exploit women, children, Blacks, the poor. It will have a certain respect for the truth, a power which created the revolution in the first place.[22]

When Camus lived in Oran doing his research (1941–42), the city was effectively then under occupation—ruled by the Nazi client government of Vichy France. Within months of his departure it would be "liberated" as the beachhead for the Allied invasion of North Africa.

He wrote *The Plague* while editor of *Combat,* the underground paper of the French resistance movement. In 1946, just the year before its publication, he presented in *Combat* a series of eight articles that comprised a longer essay eventually published as "Neither Victims Nor Executioners."[23] It is truly a classic of nonviolence (and one Berrigan also placed in our young seminarian hands).

Of that central idea itself, this narrative conversation may well be thought a seed or expression of that essay, perhaps both. There are other connections in the novel, a concern for the concreteness and clarity of language, the refusal of "obedience to abstraction," but above all the notion of a "third way." Tarrou's story, his friendship and conversation with Dr. Reiux, are emblematic.

Camus's yearning for the third way was perhaps most tested in a subsequent war. The uprising in Algeria that broke out in 1954 could well have been called "Arab Lives Matter!" A French colony since the invasion of 1830, Algeria was ruled politically by the French citizens, some one million, who were but a tenth of the population and enjoyed substantial rights and privileges withheld from the Muslim Arab majority. Camus himself, born there, like the vast majority of French Algerians dearly loved the country and wrote for human rights within a vision of Arab, Berber, Jewish, and French unity. When economic-political reform failed, the uprising brought down more repression including civilian massacre; the independence movement responded with civilian bombings. An eight-year war of terror, including torture and guillotining by the French, was begun. Camus was heartbroken. At one point he attempted to intervene, convening a group to enact a civilian truce. It too failed. He was thought naïve or was vilified by both right and left.

22. D. Berrigan, "Letter to the Weathermen," *America,* 96.

23. Camus, "Neither Victims Nor Executioners."

Perhaps his most famous essay of this period is his "Letter to an Algerian Militant," published in 1955. It follows on the massacre of thousands of Arabs by the French. Camus confesses to being on the brink of despair. "You and I, who are so alike, who share the same culture and the same hopes, who have been brothers for so long, joined in the love we both feel for our country, know that we are not enemies . . . To that end, each of us must preach peace to his own side . . . You and I both know there will be no real winners in this war and that both now and in the future we will always have to live together in the same soil." And yet, "I know from experience that to say these things today is to venture into a no man's land between hostile armies. It is to preach the folly of war as the bullets fly." Camus never saw the end of the war. Almost absurdly, he died in a car crash in 1960.[24]

Berrigan made his own foray into the conflicted geography of Middleeast war. He spoke while the bullets still flew. This was a 1973 speech in which he chastised both sides for their violence in the October-Yom Kippur war, but holding the strongest outrage (of love) for Israel, and taking severe heat for it. In a personal visitation along with Paul Mayer following, recorded conversations with many parties across borders, tables, and factions were carefully packed and mailed from Cyprus—only to promptly disappear. So a book to be based on them never materialized. His sense of betrayal, however, was strong with Palestinian leaders who claimed to him they disavowed terrorism only to strike within weeks, killing twenty-one grade-school children in west Galilee. The tale could be long.

Though not exactly parallel, one thinks also of Berrigan's other very public correspondence in matters nonviolent. While underground, and certainly with that authority, he published in *The Village Voice*, "The Letter to the Weathermen," already cited. He commends the Weather Underground for having "everything going for them" and yet choosing against it.

> You come through in public as the embodiment of the public nightmare, menacing, sinister, senseless, and violent: a spin-off of the public dread of the Panthers and Vietcong . . . But in a sense, of course, your case is more complicated because your rebellion is not the passionate consequence of the stigma of slavery. Yours is a choice.[25]

---

24. A recent book argues that the crash was orchestrated by the KGB. https://www.theguardian.com/books/2019/dec/05/albert-camus-murdered-by-the-kgb-giovanni-catelli.

25. D. Berrigan, *America*, 93.

As was his own. Following a careful discussion of Catonsville, as "tactical sabotage," he urges that "the new man and woman" "in a new world" will be nonviolent. I once had occasion to ask Bernadine Dorn and Bill Ayers of the group how they received the letter. They paused. With great appreciation they found it thoughtful, helpful, important. Though not all on the left or right counted it so.

The other public correspondence, also in the seventies, was with Ernesto Cardenal, a former Trappist novice under Merton, then participating fully in the Nicaraguan revolution. Following a published interview of Cardenal, Dan wrote in the *National Catholic Reporter* a public letter to his "dear brother." His quarrel was not with the choices of *campesinos* to take arms and rise up (though he had become convinced that nonviolent revolution was the truest way to topple dictators), but with blessing it as a practice of the Word, a way to bring on the kingdom of God, indeed an expression of the Gospel. All of these for him led unequivocally to nonviolence, but not without struggle.

> This is a long loneliness, and a thankless one. One says "no" when every ache of the heart would say "yes." We long for a community on the land, heartening liturgies, our own turf, the arts, a place where sane ecology can heal us. And the big boot comes down.[26]

It's reported that Emmanuel Mounier, lead figure in French personalism—a philosophical and theological strand beneath the Catholic Worker movement—found *The Plague* "grey and heavy."[27] He could not be held wrong. But there are moments of luminescence that break through, suggesting light held back by greyness, perhaps present as suppressed throughout. One of those occurs at the conclusion of the rooftop conversation.

> "It comes to this," Tarrou said almost casually, "what interests me is learning how to be a saint."
> "But you don't believe in God."
> "Exactly! Can one be a saint without God?—that's the only problem, I'm up against today . . ."
> "Perhaps," the doctor answered, "But, you know, I feel more fellowship with the defeated than with the saints. Heroism and sanctity don't appeal to me, I imagine. What interests me is being a man."
> "Yes, we're both after the same thing, but I'm less ambitious."[28]

26. D. Berrigan, "Killing for the Love of the Kingdom."
27. See Zaretsky, "Out of the Clear Blue Sky."
28. Camus, *Plague*, 257.

Thereupon the doctor suggests that "for friendship's sake" they should go for a swim in the sea. Both have medical passes that allow them to the docks. The swim out beneath the night sky leaves the virus or plague behind, not forgotten, but somehow escaped. Free of. There was happiness in each other's visage. "They dressed and started back. Neither said a word, but they were conscious of being perfectly one, and the memory of this night would be cherished by them both."[29] Moments such.

As a character, it was Tarrou in whom Berrigan took most interest.

> Tarrou in *The Plague* builds what we might almost call a monastic ascesis of comprehension. It would seem to be a key idea with Camus. It demands first of all a constant *attention*. The mind, in order to include the world, must come to "the still point of the turning world." Every activist, if he is not to heap chaos upon disorder, is called to contemplation.[30]

He accounted Tarrou the exemplar of modesty over against the citizenry of Oran, who so forgot to be modest. "In a more grandiose age, the word was perhaps humility; it separated the saint from the grandee, secular or sacred."[31] Or again, on that topic:

> Finally, one may be called, through this process, to become "a saint without God." Such a conception, as it seems to me, is to be translated not as a form of atheism, but as a reaction against the "reward obsession" of most Christians. To be virtuous without God is to refuse the bribe under the table.[32]

The other death that the doctor and Camus recount in painful detail is Tarrou's. I spare you it here. Suffice to say, it stemmed from the risk of the sanitary squad and the works of mercy. It all comes down to fidelity and relationship.

> Tarrou had "lost the match," as he put it. But what had he, Reiux, won? No more than the experience of having known the plague and remembered it, of knowing affection and being destined one day to remember it. So, all one could win in the conflict between

---

29. Camus, *Plague,* 257.
30. D. Berrigan, *No Bars,* 137.
31. D. Berrigan, *No Bars,* 139.
32. D. Berrigan, *No Bars,* 138.

plague and life was knowledge and memories. But Tarrou, perhaps, would have called that winning the match.[33]

Among those who exercise Tarrou's ethic and the doctor's—to be decent and human and so to do one's job—I think in this COVID period first of nurses and doctors, "essential" minimum wage workers. Here in Detroit I'm mindful of young frontline folks delivering water to those shut-off. Friends dropping food or cash on porches. Our Catholic Worker kitchen, Manna Community Meal, is kept going as a safe-distance bag-lunch food-line in the alley behind the church, at the hands of Fa. Tom Lumpkin, eighty, and Marianne Arbogast, along with a handful of young new Catholic Workers from Day House (whose reading helped shape these reflections). I think on Workers all over the country doing some version of the same. And yes, friends continuing to resist war in the midst of pandemic and uprising. The blessing of Dorothy Day, Daniel Berrigan and Albert Camus, along with Dr. Rieux and Saint Tarrou, be upon them all.

33. Camus, *Plague*, 291.

Aside from Voices (A Letter from Kathy Kelly)

December 20, 2020

Dear Bill,

Warm greetings from Chicagoland on a relatively uncluttered Sunday morning, one that allowed plenty of time for reading and study, and led to this letter.

Mainly, I want to express gratitude. Thank you, Bill, for cultivating your unusual, valuable trove of memories regarding mentors, especially Dan Berrigan, who helped shape your life.

I was a junior in high school when I "met" Dan through a bookstore. If I caught the express bus into downtown Chicago, following my last class of the day, I could arrive fifteen minutes early for my job at a shoe store on State Street and spend time browsing at St. Benet's, a Catholic, left-leaning shop selling books, posters, and art work. For about two years, the two women running the place steadily acquainted me with writings of Catholic radicals. I was easily enamored with Dan's handsome magnetism and banner-worthy one-liners. Resisting war and racism seemed almost otherworldly to me; civil disobedience exotic beyond belief. And the thought of ever meeting the Berrigans never crossed my mind. But I was hooked, long distance.

I confess to a twinge of envy regarding the deep, personal friendships you and others developed with Dan. Yet, while not part of a more intimate inner circle, I did, for a time, dwell with a group whose connection with Dan had become, for a time, a matter of life and death.

We were peace activists who had come to a desert encampment in a remote area of Iraq to be part of the Gulf Peace Team. It was January, 1991, and we expected the US to bomb and invade Iraq "any day." Organizers of the team had called for participants to interpose themselves between the warring parties. We were uncertain what "interpositioning" would turn out to be, but all of us were certain about risking our lives, if need be, for the sake of interfering with the war against Iraq. What led seventy people from eighteen different countries to that unusual circle?

I remember being amazed that so many team members spoke of Dan when talking about their reason for being there. Two women, Anne Montgomery and Kathy Boylan, were friends with Dan. Both were seasoned Plowshares activists. But most of the group had never met him.

Even so, people repeatedly spoke of being influenced by Dan's assertion that one of the reasons we don't have peace is because people give only a half of their life to peace. Soldiers go to war knowing it might cost them their lives. Do peace activists trying to prevent war expect as much of themselves? People who volunteered to join the Gulf Peace Team had gotten and shared Dan's message. Somehow I felt he was essentially on the team, deeply related to all of us.

I cherish a particular memory of Dan. Toward the end of his life, he had come to a liturgy at Mary House Catholic Worker in New York City. When it was time to exchange the kiss of peace, Dan sat while each person in the room approached him. I can only describe his expression as beatific. Radiantly happy, with hands outstretched as though beholding a marvelous work of art, Dan greeted each person in the room.

This morning I watched a video of a speech you gave at Loyola University a few years ago, when you were asked to talk about friendship between Daniel Berrigan and William Stringfellow. At the podium you had well-worn, marked copies of books by both of them. I marveled at how easily you could move between passages from these books and stories about your own personal encounters with "Dan" and "Bill." You quote Merton in a letter to a young activist (Jim Forest), saying: "It is the reality of personal relationships that saves everything."

Dan and Phil summoned people to save a world afflicted by the pestilence of war and the omnicidal threat of nuclear weapons. They were up against monumentally dehumanizing and destructive forces. As you describe their pursuit of peacemaking, we see, repeatedly, the "gamble" Albert Camus describes in his essay "Neither Victims nor Executioners." We are in history up to our necks, Camus says, but he recommends waging the formidable gamble that words are stronger than weapons.

I wonder if, in this time of pandemic, Camus might be revived as a mentor for innumerable people and communities who look to *The Plague* for insights. It's interesting to think of how much importance Camus assigned to relationships as he developed the characters in *The Plague*.

Jean Tarrou joins Dr. Rieux in his endeavor to "save the world," in this case the small Algerian town of Oran. Their deepening relationship helps them persist with difficult, everyday work of combating the bubonic plague. Meanwhile, the townspeople become increasingly lifeless, indifferent, and bored. The plague had "killed off not only the faculty of love but even of friendship."

You call attention to a tantalizingly beautiful section of the novel that tells of a night when Dr. Rieux and Tarrou decide to escape the town and go for a swim in the ocean. Camus may want readers to think of the two saviors being baptized together. They experience a sense of joyful oneness afterward. And, seemingly fortified, they return to their exhausting work.

I think *The Plague* offers a clear message: salvation comes from acting out of human decency, to be decent and human, and so to do one's job, trying always to save children from torture. I think Camus would have agreed with Merton, relationships "save everything."

Count on your audience, Bill, whether listeners or readers, to store your words and stories. Be assured that gratitude for these stories connects people.

An indigenous botanist and author, Robin Kimmerer, writes beautifully about gratitude prompting people to make gifts in return. She describes a reciprocity that becomes a truly renewable resource.

Speaking of renewable resourcefulness, let me also thank you for recalling, in your talk at Loyola, the action of the Kings Bay Plowshares Seven. When you spoke, they were awaiting trial. You noted that one of them, a Jesuit priest, Steve Kelly, remained in a county jail. As I write, Steve is still jailed. My next letters will be to Carmen and Martha, now completing their first of many weeks in federal prison.

That commitment to "other-preservation" rather than self-preservation (one of Martin Luther King's themes), plus assurance you can't kill the spirit, will be ours to carry forth. The beautiful line from Hebrews 12:1 comes to mind: "Surrounded by so great a cloud of witnesses . . ."

Gratefully,
Kathy

> *Kathy Kelly is a peace activist, pacifist, and author. Believing "where you stand determines what you see," her efforts have sometimes led her into war zones, jails, and prisons.*

— Chapter 9 —

Friend: Berrigan with Stringfellow

And so many thanks for the good enclosures. [Bill's] writings are like a hot sunrise out of a grave. What thunder in the midst of the soft-soap & hard nosed bullshit we are commonly afflicted with from "church" . . . I hope the new year brings you (and by strong implication usns) closer to having the S'fellow works back on shelves, in hands & pulpits & convents & missions & even adjacent to toilet bowls (where B. often did extensive reading . . .)— Letter from Daniel, December 14, 1991[1]

GOOD EVENING![2] IT'S AN honor to be here, I'm very grateful to Michael Murphy and the Hank Center for the invitation. And also to the Center just for recognizing the importance of Dan Berrigan's life and work in, let us say, Catholic intellectual thought and heritage.

Sixty years of word and deed, in his case, is bearing fruit now, under Francis. The just war theory is being upended, gospel nonviolence is actually being embraced, and in a certain sense, Daniel's life and work with the communities of which he was part, undergird that and yield it. Berrigan week is right on time in exactly that sense.

Because of both the exhibit that the folks on Block Island have pulled together and the short film *Seeking Shelter* by Sue Hagadorn that will be showing tomorrow evening,[3] I have titled my remarks for the evening "William Stringfellow and Daniel Berrigan: The Politics of Friendship."

---

1. D. Berrigan to Wylie-Kellermann, author's files. The book in question which came to be was *Keeper*. See also Wylie-Kellermann, ed., *Essential*.

2. A video of the original presentation may be seen at https://www.youtube.com/watch?list=PLDVJZ3DnYTd9EfJ2jSzTM_tCUmW1ftIC2&v=xZcLo9HDjRQ&feature=emb_title.

3. Hagadorn, dir., *Seeking Shelter*.

I want to begin with a text. It's a paragraph from a long letter, many of you will know this, which Thomas Merton wrote to Jim Forest, who's recently the biographer of Dan Berrigan and at one time was a hoped-to-be speaker in this week. Forest was in 1966 a staff member of the Catholic Peace Fellowship and had at the time fallen into certain despair about his work, which he conveyed to Merton. And so the Trappist monk and hermit wrote him a long letter. I'm just going to read a paragraph of it. It's somewhat widely known . . . I think some of you may recognize it. I notice it in blogs and posters and clippings tacked above young people's computer screens. And it's best known as "A Letter to a Young Activist."

> And then this: do not depend on the hope of results. When you are doing the sort of work you have taken on, essentially an apostolic work, you may have to face the fact that your work will be apparently worthless and even achieve no result at all, if not perhaps results opposite to what you expect. As you get used to this idea you start more and more to concentrate not on the results but on the value, the rightness, the truth of the work itself. And there too a great deal has to be gone through, as gradually you struggle less and less for an idea and more and more for specific people. The range tends to narrow down, but it gets much more real. In the end, as you yourself mention in passing, it is the reality of personal relationships that saves everything.[4]

In the end, things come down to relationship, to friendship, to community.

Since I'm the first speaker in the series, I wonder if it's incumbent on me to say something about who Dan Berrigan is. I can be brief. He's a Jesuit priest, an award-winning poet, a convicted federal felon twice over. He was an author of fifty books, all of them theological, if you will. Some are essay and journal-like books, particularly those that were written in prison or in his time underground on the lam. But the majority are either poetry or biblical commentary. And those latter volumes cover all of the prophets systematically, as well as the Apocalypse of John, plus volumes on Jesus and Paul. None are what you could properly call critical works, though he was well-read in the critical literature. But his writing was much more engaged, if you will, explicit about the social location from which he and his community read the book and entered into a biblical conversation. And that

---

4. Forest, *Root* 192–93.

was a place of nonviolent resistance to empire, which is to say, neither a safe nor completely objective reading of the text.

That's also to say, that along with his brother Philip, he virtually pioneered new forms of nonviolent action which I've taken to calling "liturgical direct action." Action which is public, ritualized, sacramental, and prayerful. In a certain sense it reflected and arose from experience of the Second Vatican Council. Let's call it opening out liturgy and sacrament to the world. So, for example, in 1968, it was the notorious draft board raid in Catonsville, Maryland, where he and eight others, including Philip, went into the draft board, and removed 1A files of people who were about to be sent to Vietnam. These they took to the parking lot, and burned with homemade napalm, surrounding the fire with a circle of prayer, of repentance. Dorothy Day, who had qualms about the action initially, in an address to the Liturgical Conference, referred to it as an act of prayer. William Stringfellow later called it a politically informed exorcism.

The action was replicated in other draft board raids across the county, including one here in Chicago—you may know as the Chicago Fifteen. When I was a college student, I had a poster on my dorm wall, I don't know if it was a Corita Kent or not, but it was a very brightly colored orange and yellow poster of flames. They had acted on Pentecost, so the text of the poster was from Acts 2: "These men are not drunk as you imagine, it's only the third hour of the day." Forgive me, I'm going sideways very quickly here . . . Later, I had a conversation with Joe Mulligan, a Jesuit priest who was part of that action, and I told him about that poster. He said that actually they were drunk [laughter]. He told how they had to wait outside the draft board all night, and it was bitterly cold, and friends kept bringing hot toddies, so by the morning they were nearly tipsy when they finally went in.

But returning to Daniel, twelve years later, in 1980, again with Philip and six others, he entered a General Electric plant in Pennsylvania where nuclear warheads were being made, and literalized Isaiah's prophesy to beat swords into plowshares. They used hammers to damage and unmake or remake the weapons. Just as Catonsville spawned a hundred other draft board actions in this country, so too the Plowshares Eight action has likewise proliferated several decades of similar actions. The most recent took place in Kings Bay, Georgia, at the Trident submarine base on April 4, the anniversary of Dr. King's assassination. Liz McAllister, wife and partner of Phil, in the Jonah House community, was one of those who cut the fence, used hammers, and poured blood. They specifically acted to face what Dr. King, in a speech the year prior on April 4, called the Giant Triplets of racism, militarism, and extreme materialism. I hope you're aware that the Poor People's Campaign, which has an organization here in Chicago, has picked up the work King was doing then and is addressing these, adding a fourth, a quadruplet—ecological injustice and devastation. Martin King held that a revolution of values was required if they were to be overcome. Liz McAlister, of that group, is one of two currently in jail, awaiting trial to begin shortly.

Daniel died two years ago, just shy of ninety-five. Some of you may have been at the funeral. I was honored not only to be part of the procession from the Catholic Worker to the church but be asked to say a few words at the wake the night before at St. Francis Xavier.

I met him when I was a seminary student in New York at Union in 1972. He had just been released from Danbury prison for the Catonsville action, and came to New York to teach. I was in his class on the book of Revelation and Jacques Ellul, the French biblical theologian and social historian, who both Bill Stringfellow and Dan were very taken with. I'd grown up in an evangelical church and held the Bible in high regard, but no one read the book with life-and-death seriousness the way that he did. *Everything* was staked on this. And I kind of freaked in. I realized I was going through a conversion after I was already in seminary, and he noticed. I have a vivid memory of him calling my name down the hall and inviting me up for scotch and then, you know, come back on Tuesday for some tea. And suddenly I'm meeting with him a couple times a week, and like any good evangelical I'd never heard of spiritual direction, but I'd been drawn into it, and suddenly he's putting Dorothy Day and Merton books in my hand. He knew how to take young people under his wing. That was the beginning not only of a serious mentorship but a lifelong friendship.

Now I'm thinking of the two, Dan and Bill, and it's probably Stringfellow who I need to say the more about. As a college student in the forties, he was internationally known in the ecumenical student Christian movement. Which really was a movement, indeed a global movement at the time. Later, when he, "suffered a conversion" by reading the Bible in the army, in Germany, he came to look back on the student years as more than a little pharisaical. He'd been what he called a professional Christian, making a career of religious leadership. As a consequence, he said he died to career, which he regarded itself among the principalities and powers.

In 1956, he graduated from Harvard Law School and so was poised for a lucrative career, right? Instead he made for East Harlem, where he lived and did street law before there was such a thing, before there was a legal services corporation or any of that, with the support of the East Harlem Protestant Parish. That move to the margin, many of his friends thought, was a bad career move.

But there, in East Harlem, because of the way folks on the street spoke about The Man or the cops, or the welfare bureaucracy, or the absentee landlords, or the philanthropic enterprises, as though they were predatory creatures arrayed against the community, he began to pay attention to the New Testament language of the principalities and powers, which had become obscure and opaque to most Christians. That was because, hermeneutically, as far back as the fourth century, they had been projected into spiritual outer space. The words "rulers, authorities, dominions, thrones" were regarded as having no political reference. You could name some historical moments, one was resistance to Hitler and Nazism, where suddenly people are paying attention to these terms in a new and concrete way. And Stringfellow was one of those who helped bring the principalities back onto the map of Christian social ethics. Much like Daniel Berrigan, he was never fully embraced by the academy. Stringfellow, even though he had a huge influence with respect to the powers, people would read him, use his stuff, but remain unacknowledged and unfootnoted. Yet he really shaped what was a restructuring of New Testament language. Walter Wink, who has done so much recent work on the principalities, said he reread Bill's work and was embarrassed by how much Stringfellow he'd been uttering without crediting or even realizing it—the insights and material had just gotten into his thought.

Here in Chicago, at the University of Chicago Rockefeller Chapel, Stringfellow, an attorney, was the only non-academically trained theologian who queried Karl Barth, the Protestant Swiss theologian in his one visit to America. Stringfellow's questions (it was a genuine conversation) were substantially about the principalities. They concerned the state, in Romans 13, explicitly about the Confessing Church resistance movement in Germany. At the end of the exchange, Karl Barth stood up, looked at the audience, and said, "You should listen to this man."

And then the following year, in 1963, at the Edgewater Hotel—you know the big pink building which rises where Sheridan turns into Lake Shore Drive—the first national conference on religion and race was held.

Martin Luther King was the headliner at that. Rabbi Abraham Heschel was the keynoter to the week. And Stringfellow was the respondent to Heschel. And he said a number of things that stirred controversy. But the most substantial one had to do with naming white supremacy as a demon, as a principality. I'll read to you; this is in the book that Michael's making available, these are part of his remarks:

> From the point of view of either Biblical religion, the monstrous American heresy is in thinking that the whole drama of history takes places between God and human beings. But the truth Biblically and theologically and empirically is quite otherwise. The drama of this history takes place among God and human beings and the principalities and powers. The great institutions and ideologies active in the world. It's the corruption and shallowness of humanism which beguiles Jew or Christian into believing that human beings are masters of institutions or ideology. Or to put it a bit differently: racism is not an evil in human hearts or minds. Racism is a principality, a demonic power, a representative image, an embodiment of death, over which human beings have little or no control but which works its awful influence over their lives.[5]

Now, don't miss the paradox here in his next line: "This is the power with which Jesus Christ was confronted and which at great and personal cost, he overcame."

A few years later, because of radical illness, Stringfellow relocated with his partner, Anthony Towne, to Block Island. He moved from Manhattan, and that was a move that would figure prominently in his friendship and the saga with Dan. From there, in an environment which he termed "monastic," he wrote his most substantial books on the powers. It was that short step off of "America," he said, off of the United States, off the edge, that seemed to enable him to size up the nation in its apocalyptic guise as Babylon. And no one's written theology more cogently about American Empire than Stringfellow. This is from an introduction to *Conscience and Obedience*:

> The effort is to comprehend the nation, to grasp what is happening right here and now to the nation, and to consider the destiny of the nation within the scope and style of the ethics and the ethical metaphors distinctive to the Biblical witness in history. The task here is to treat the nation within the tradition of Biblical politics, to understand America Biblically. Not the other way

5. Wylie-Kellermann, ed., *Essential,* 179.

around: not, to put it in an appropriately awkward way, to con-
strue the Bible American-ly.[6]

Dan and Bill met as writers. And their friendship was fertile soil
for their writing conversation. In terms of the meeting itself, Dan had
a manuscript, *They Call Us Dead Men,* which substantially, if obliquely,
reflected his experience at the Gethsemani retreat that Thomas Merton
had called in 1964, on the spiritual roots of protest. And several of the
essays, particularly on technology, came directly out of that conversation.
There were parts of the book reflecting material that he himself presented
at the retreat. Dan had read Bill's book about his experience in East Harlem called *My People is the Enemy,* and it prompted him to send him a
thank you note for the book, but also to inquire if he would write a little
introduction, a few pages for the beginning of this new manuscript, introducing it. Dan wrote me about their meeting.

> As to the intro he did to an early book of mine, when I wrote to
> ask him the favor he said "Why not come over for supper?" Their
> eyrie was just across Central Park. I went and that started things
> that never, thank God, end. Did you know by the way (perfectly
> useless intelligence) they were raising rabbits, tomatoes & corn
> on their terrace? As to the former proliferations, neighbors com-
> plained & the city health dep't arrived. Shortly, the wabbits went
> where the woodbine twineth.[7]

He also wrote:

> The two dwelt in a penthouse atop a run down building on the
> Upper West side . . . The ample rooms had a lived in, doggy look
> . . . Heady years, people forever coming and going. Among church
> folk of migratory proclivities, there arose an unspoken dogma; the
> Stringfellonian menage and management were to be accounted
> among the prime sights and sounds of the city. Not to be missed!
> The gyrovague Christians arrived, hot after the spoor of the fa-
> mous author, theologian, Harlem Lawyer. They came and came.
> Bill was, alas, constitutionally unable to say nay . . . Domestic par-
> tying was frequent. There was a hilarious all-night auction of art, a
> fundraiser for SNCC or CORE. Corita Kent donated several of her

---

6. Wylie-Kellermann, ed., *Essential,* 45.
7. Berrigan to Wylie-Kellermann, Thanksgiving, 1991.

incomparable serigraphs, but the non-stop pace was taking a steep toll. Bill was losing weight and failing alarmingly.[8]

Stringfellow's introduction to Dan's book signaled how quickly their friendship had taken. He began: "This passionate one, this meek poet, this exemplary human being, this priest of Christ now gives us a wise, lucid, compelling and edifying testament affirming the sacramental integrity of human life in this world."[9]

I'm mindful that we gather within weeks of the fiftieth anniversary of the Catonsville trial. Each evening after the courtroom was adjourned, people would move to St. Ignatius church and there would be held what was called a festival of life. Beyond the long reach of the law was poetry and music and preaching and doxology and art. And there Stringfellow appeared. He was then at the peak of his illness and would shortly undergo radical surgery. He struggled to climb into the pulpit and this is what he rose to say:

> Remember, now, that the state has only one power it can use against you, against human beings: death. The state can persecute you, prosecute you, imprison you, exile you, execute you, all of these mean the same thing. The state can consign you to death. The grace of Jesus Christ in this life is that death fails. There is nothing the state can do to you or to me which we need fear.[10]

He was stunned when the congregation burst into a standing ovation and then broke into song.

The trial actually did issue in a deadly guilty verdict, and within weeks Dan was at Stringfellow's bedside in Manhattan, where finally his illness had been accurately diagnosed. He decided to undergo radical experimental surgery, which the doctors were uncertain would work, or even that he would survive. His pancreas was be removed, which would render him a complete diabetic, dependent on animal enzymes for digestion, less all the functions that the pancreas normally plays. When Dan was at his bedside, Bill, following the trial, was lamenting he wasn't able to participate in actions of civil disobedience. Dan said to him, "Your illness is your imprisonment." And Stringfellow replied, "Yes, my preparation for concentration camp." His humor was wry.

---

8. D. Berrigan, "My Friend," 100–101.

9. Stringfellow, "Introduction" to D. Berrigan, *Dead Men*, 11.

10. Stringfellow, *Second Birthday*, 133.

There were appeals of verdict in the year that followed, but at a certain point the Nine were supposed to turn themselves in for their sins. On the day that Dan was supposed to submit, he organized a big festival, public event, at Cornell, called America is Hard to Find. So, he's up on stage speaking, and the federal marshals guarding all the exits are nervous that he's not going to do this and submit. Up on stage are giant puppets with people inside from the Bread and Puppet Theater, if you know that troupe. It was the twelve apostles on stage behind him, bringing their apostolic witness. And at a certain point one of the puppets leaned over to Dan and said, "Do you want to get out of here?" And he said, "Sure!" and a moment later, the lights went out, the puppeteer handed over his get up. Dan went inside the giant likeness of Peter or John or whomever it was; the lights came back on, and Dan was gone. The puppets went back out the door and into a van for a hasty getaway.

Berrigan was underground for five months, evading capture, living on the Ten Most Wanted list of the FBI, driving J. Edgar Hoover berserk. He would pop up at well-known pulpits, preach a sermon about resistance, and disappear. He would be on national television and slip out the back door. And that became, well, exhausting at a certain point. At a certain point he made overtures through the underground network, would he be welcome at Stringfellow's place on Block Island? He hopped the ferry and went. Down the hill from Bill's house lived his neighbor, "the Commodore," who was very supportive of the government and thought the FBI could do anything they damn well wanted. Bill and Anthony later found, on the wall of their neighbor's house, a wooden platform that seemed to have been constructed as suitable for aiming a directional microphone at their picture window, where the dining room table sat. There Bill and Dan and Anthony talked during his visit. We once tried to FOIA to see if there's an FBI transcript of those conversations, but it's never turned up . . . It would be weirdly lovely if there were.

I do know several things about which they talked. Dan went underground on April 9, which is the anniversary of Dietrich Bonhoeffer's execution by the Nazis. On the run, he began reading Eberhard Bethge's biography of Bonhoeffer, and wrote a poetic review of it that appeared in *The Saturday Review*. One of the topics they discussed was Bonhoeffer's Underground Seminary at Finkenwalde, which was a resistance seminary in the late thirties. Dan and Bill wondered aloud whether it was possible to create such an underground seminary in this country. They considered

Block Island as a possible place, with its hotels virtually empty during the off-season school year. In any event, that was a conversation that eventually connected with my experience and story with them. Their other topic of discussion was the book of Revelation. Both of them were really taken with the import of that for understanding the present historical moment. It was that which Dan was teaching when he came out of Danbury, to Union, and Bill's next book, *An Ethic for Christians and Other Aliens in a Strange Land*, drew closely on the Babylon parables of Revelation.

Dan tells the story, I hope you get to see him do so in the film tomorrow, of the FBI coming disguised as birdwatchers and arresting him. He prevented them from getting into the house, for which he was glad. Oh, I was going to say a third thing they may have talked about. Dan was staying in a little out building that Bill and Anthony called the manger, formerly a little animal stable, for a donkey or something. It had been fixed up as Anthony's study and Dan used it as his writing place and abode for those days. Eventually, Bill and Anthony arranged to have built a cottage for Dan on the bluffs overlooking the Atlantic. It was really his hermitage, his escape place from Manhattan, though he also offered it to other people fresh out of prison for recuperation . . . my wife and I honeymooned there. He was very generous with it, but it was also his kind of hiding place. It's possible they may have first talked about whether something like that was feasible.

After Dan's capture, Bill and Anthony were indicted for harboring a fugitive, charged with a felony. I have here their statement following that indictment:

> Daniel Berrigan is our friend. We rejoice in that fact and strive to be worthy of it. Our hospitality to Daniel Berrigan is no crime. At a certain time and in a certain place we did "relieve, receive, comfort and assist" him and we did "offer and give sustenance and lodging" to him. We did not "harbor" or "conceal" him. We did not "hinder" the authorities. Father Berrigan has and had no need to be concealed. By his own extraordinary vocation, and by the grace of God, he has become one of the conspicuous Christians of these wretched times. We have done what we could do to affirm him in this regard. We categorically deny that we have done anything to conceal him. We are not disposed to hide what light there is under a bushel.[11]

---

11. Stringfellow and Towne, "A Statement by the Accused."

The Block Island Two were in effect being prosecuted for practicing the Christian virtue of hospitality, which I believe Bill sort of delighted in. No need to lament any incapacity for civil resistance. Anthony, on the other hand, given Bill's still-frail health situation, was irate: "They're trying to kill him—they're trying to kill Bill." If their response in the statement sounds extraordinary, think of the host of underground safehouses where night after night Berrigan was met with friendship and risky hospitality, virtually improvising an underground network of communities, of relationship and bonds. Effectively a community of resistance and resurrection. I once heard someone ask Bill what exactly he meant by "resurrection." And he paused a beat and he said, "Dan Berrigan in prison." What seemed really cryptic at the time, I later heard him elaborate on. He reflected at length on a visit he made to the prisoners at Danbury, how there he beheld the witness of the resurrection, specifically in Berrigan's demeanor. He told of arranging the visit and how the warden and the other authorities, even the chaplain, had seemed constrained, anxious, dehumanized, unfree in the fulfillment of their functions, unable to make the most ordinary decisions without consulting the Attorney General. Whereas the prisoners, on the other hand, Dan and Phil, though certainly inconvenienced by their confinement, seemed truly free and joyful and unconstrained, unencumbered by the location. This he thought represented the radical freedom of the resurrection.

Bill and Anthony wrote to Dan and Philip about the blocks they were encountering to a prison visitation as well as their own dire, if temporary, straits:

> It may be some comfort for you to know that the walls around you are harder to get in through than they are to get out through. We have tried to get in. Lord knows we have tried. Neither our persons nor our missives have been found compatible with your rehabilitation to society. Your keepers will not allow us to interrupt your smooth progress back into the company of decent folk. For a time there seemed a good chance we might join you behind the walls by the processes which are by law provided. We were moved to the edge of the community and seemed to be programed for the outer darkness. A benevolent judge, however, discerning a mote in our accuser's eye, decreed the mote would have to be cast out first. We are left meanwhile in the inner darkness which thickens daily all about us.[12]

12. Letter undated (probably from 1971) from Stringfellow and Towne to Daniel and Philip in Danbury Federal Correctional, in the "Stringfellow Files," Cornell University

Stringfellow died in 1985 of the cumulative effects of diabetes. In his will (I should've brought it along) he left me his New Testament, the one that he read in the army that prompted his conversion. When Daniel preached the funeral on the Island, the New Testament was indeed in the procession and on the altar. Dan's remarks included testimony to their friendship. "This was the aspect of Christ that this Christian kept opening before his friends. Christ was our friend, in such a world, in such a lifetime as ours, precisely because He does not betray."[13]

I close with a poem of Dan's to Bill:

My Last Death was William Stringfellow's.[14]

Death
rattled its begging bowl
like the drummer of Armageddon.
Sustenance! Sympathy! it drummed

Stringfellow bethought; Death
lacking a name—
(Unnameable, nameless horror
they muttered in terror)—
he named it finally, taming
once for all
the appetite that fed
on kings and clowns—
fed and fed, never satiated—
women, warriors, the sleepy eyed unborn—
never enough!

We must break this thrall
once for all, became his mind's
holy obsession and vocation.

Like a priest's crucifix aloft
before the obscene undead,
Christ expiring for love, summoning a last
commanding cry; Down dog death!—

Archives.

13. D. Berrigan, "A Homiletical Afterword," in Wylie-Kellermann, ed., *Essential*, 231–34.

14. D. Berrigan, "Death and Life of a Friend," in *Risen Bread*, 297–98.

Thus Stringfellow. Transfixed, laid claim
years and years, a crucifix in hands
not his, miraculous he moved in the world
chasing death pitilessly
dismaying, dispelling death.

Then as the sun advances, and shadows
go underground
he stands, believe, in resplendent noon.
Taken from the cross
he ascends straight up.

And death, shadowy, starved, named
for what it is, is not
and nowhere to be seen.

Friendly Aside: At Door and Table
(A Letter from Jim Reale)

Dear Bill,

It will be five years on April 30th that Dan died. Below is the circuitous map as to how I met Dan, and his influence that led me from Island laborer to activist, federal prisoner, yoga teacher, hospice nurse, and documentary filmmaker.

My connection to Dan began in the fall of 1984, when I received a call from the women in Block Island's Catholic community. They were calling on behalf of Bill Stringfellow, who lived alone and was not in good health. They requested I move in with him and be his caretaker. I had heard of Bill around the Island. A lawyer and writer. He was a tiny man I would occasionally see in the Post Office. He called me one day and invited me to have breakfast at Ernie's Restaurant in Old Harbor. We met and he asked, "Do you know why they want you to move in?" "Well, I suppose you may need help with some heavy work around the house," I said. "No" Bill replied. "They don't want to find me dead and stinking a week later." My eggs over easy no longer looked appetizing.

I moved in soon after.

On a bright sunny day the following month I came home from my job laboring for a mason, exhausted and covered with cement dust. A stranger opened the door and said, "Welcome," hand extended. I thought to myself, "I live here . . . and who are you?" It was Daniel Berrigan, come for a visit to see how Stringfellow was faring. The three of us had dinner for several evenings. They were talking politics and theology while I was primarily focused on the chow, scratching my head and debating if I should leave after dinner and go to the local watering hole to shoot some Eight Ball. I was still working on my long rail bank shots.

Bill died in the spring of 1985 in a hospital on the mainland from complications of diabetes.

I became the caretaker of the two houses for several years. Dan would visit at least twice a year and we would have dinner in his cottage (Stringfellow gave him lifetime access in his will) during his seven–to–ten-day getaway. I found his life and stories so different than mine. He was getting arrested for an end to nuclear weapons, participating in anti-war demonstrations, going to jail, teaching peace and nonviolence in universities and serving the AIDS community. Clearly, he wasn't working on his bank shots.

It was the summer of 1987 on Block Island, and Dan had cooked yet another fabulous supper at the cottage. We were sitting at a small square card table where we had dinner, overlooking the ocean at bluff's edge facing east. We were alone. I was twenty-seven and still hadn't found my way in the world outside of surviving as a construction worker and arborist. It was particularly late in the evening and we had "cracked a jar" earlier that night. After much conversation, as one can imagine with Daniel Berrigan, something came over me. In that tiny two-room house, fist pounding the table, without warning, I yelled out desperately with Dan as my witness, "I don't know what to do with my life. What does God want of me?" Dan reached over and held my hand to comfort. Not a word. Simply his reassuring gesture and bowed head, as he met my angst with the great wisdom of silence and friendship.

Friendship was a very important part of Dan's life. His understanding of friendship was biblical rather than casual—"I have called you friends." Dan was a friend of Jesus because he did the works of the Prince of Peace: extraordinary peacemaking, working with the dying, teaching nonviolence, rejecting the swords of our time (guns, bombs, wars), bringing people together, sitting down for a meal with friends and strangers, confronting injustice, witnessing against the powers of state and religious institutions that oppress the marginalized, and living in community. It was a long list that Dan continued to work on throughout his life.

One may be tempted to assume that Dan was amassing an army of anti-war activists to carry out his vision of peace through civil disobedience. Not so. He wasn't a recruiter for any cause, however needed or noble. Nor was he fixed on making his purpose your purpose. More accurate to say, he was a pied piper for peace and disarmament. You either heard his music or not. It was more his conviction rather than any effort to convince you that created a turning of one's life in a direction other than self. He was able to focus on an individual much like a teacher from the East mentors a student, with great care and a deep understanding of the qualities and abilities unique to the person in front of him. This is the side of Daniel Berrigan not known publicly: his wise contemplative heart woven with love for God, people, earth.

Dan meditated on biblical writings most of his life. Yoga philosophy contends, if you "direct the mind exclusively towards an object and sustain that direction without distraction" the mind reflects the object like a clear and perfect mirror. For Dan his object was the Scripture, both Old and New Testament. And so he resembled, he reflected, he became Scripture. The story and life of Jesus continues through those who imitate Jesus's actions.

But Dan wasn't preachy. He taught the example of Jesus in a way that was not religious but human. Down to earth, give-a-damn-for-your-fellow-man-and-woman, human. Consider everyone as yourself. If you are able to approach life with this fundamental Christian teaching and you happen to also justify war and the civilian deaths that it breeds, then you must add yourself and all those you love into the carnage of past, present, and future wars. Then take a good look and determine if this is the moral compass you wish to be guided by. The biblical teaching, "Do unto others as you would have them do unto you" is blindsided by love for country, power, and amnesia for forgiveness and mercy.

Dan placed himself in the shoes of the disenfranchised, the poor, those under war, the hungry, the homeless, the prisoner, the addict, the dying, and said, "How can I treat any of these with less regard than myself?" This daily meditation is what guided him.

Justice is a contagion. Dan transmitted justice. If you were with him for any length of time you caught the justice bug and the way you saw and acted in the world would change for the rest of your life.

Because of Dan's example, I left Block Island to live with Phil Berrigan, Liz McAllister, Frida, Jerry, Kate, and other adults at Jonah House in Baltimore. A community based on nonviolence, disarmament, and solidarity with the poor. Guided by Jesus as the quintessential activist in all of history. These influences led me to a Plowshares action, federal prison, a 2,500-mile bicycle pilgrimage to El Salvador, and a peacekeeping witness in Bosnia during the war.

After these rather challenging, demanding years, I knew I needed some respite so I went to a yoga center to become a yoga teacher. Dan had no connection to yoga, but because he believed in me and our decades-long friendship, he gave me a check for 1,000 dollars to pay for the training. Some years later, my life changed again: I went to school to become a hospice nurse, partly due to Dan's influence in working with the dying and my father's own death. And just six years ago, I was called out of the blue by Sue Hagedorn, asking if I'd like to be involved in making a short documentary on Dan and Stringfellow, titled *Seeking Shelter*. After that, I went on to work with her on a full-length film, *The Berrigans Devout and Dangerous*.

Never could I have predicted how the stranger at my door some thirty-eight years ago would have changed my life in ways unimaginable.

I saw Dan three days before his last Christmas at Murray-Weigel Hall in the Bronx. He was nearly nonverbal and it would be only a few short months before his death. He sat in his wheel chair while I, on bent knee before him, clasped his hands. Looking downward and inward with a monastic silence, we entered into a contemplative state I shall never forget. And so I dare to say, if you have met Daniel Berrigan you have met Christ, because he dwelt within him.

I am reminded of the yoga master T. K. V. Desikachar in Chennai, India, who said, "A teacher takes the hand, opens the mind, and most importantly touches the heart."

This is what Daniel Berrigan did for me.

Many thanks, Bill, for the friendship we share and the common heart we inherited from Dan.

Jim Reale

Jim Reale, sixty-two, is a hospice nurse for the last ten years, Plowshares activist, filmmaker, yoga teacher, and certified yoga therapist. He teaches retreats nationally, integrating Eastern contemplative practice and Western spirituality with a focus on chanting. He lives in Albuquerque, New Mexico with his wife Barbara Stavola.

—— Chapter 10 ——

Contemplative: An Urban Hermit's Place on the Bluff

PPS. Come out here in winter. It might be a Trappist cloister, just so q-u-i-e-t. love yez, Daniel[1] from the Island, November 1998.

SILENCE. A TRAPPIST DISCIPLINE. A Zen practice. A pause of breath in the poet's verse.

During Nixon's 1972 Christmas bombing of North Vietnam, Dan sat with Thich Nhat Hanh[2] outside of Paris to talk. Jim Forest, friend and now biographer, was along. His published account began with the following note:

> A great deal is missing from the transcription—not in words but most of all in the silences between them. Between Dan's opening comments and Nhat Hanh's first response was a silence that seemed ten minutes long, a complete stillness in which it was easy to hear the slight noise of the Sony tape recorder. Silence remained enough a part of the conversation to make of both of them honorary Quakers or Trappists or similar sorts of heretics in this noisy, clock-centered world.[3]

Dan returned to New York to resume teaching our little seminary band. The prior semester, fresh from jail, he had cited Jacques Ellul to the effect that contemplation was the one thing the state could not manage or co-opt. It was an encouragement, but arguable—as he himself now pointed out in conversation with the Vietnamese Zen master.

1. D. Berrigan to Wylie-Kellermann, November 17, 1998.

2. Nhat Hanh had gone to Paris with a Buddhist delegation to be a presence at the peace talks. He was not only marginalized there, but exiled from his own country, denied re-entry, first by the South and then by the North.

3. Forest, ed., "Contemplation," 4.

So in a time when a machine is claiming its victories over men and women, it seems to me that contemplation becomes a form of resistance—and should lead to resistance in the world. And this to the point where one cannot claim [to be] in touch with God, and still be neutral toward the machine, toward the death of people. I mention this because this also is not clear, and in the derangement of our culture we see that people move toward contemplation in despair—even though unrecognized. They meditate as a way of becoming neutral—to put a guard between themselves and the horror around them, instead of allowing them to give themselves to people and to hope, instead of presenting something different, something new, to suffering people. We have a terrible kind of drug called "contemplation." The practitioners may call themselves Jesus freaks or followers of Krishna or Buddha; they may wear robes of some kind, be in the street, and beg, and pray, and live in communes, but they care nothing about the war. Nothing about the war. And they talk somewhat like Billy Graham; "Jesus saves." That is to say: it's not necessary to do anything. So they become another resource of the culture instead of a resource against the culture.[4]

Dan is best understood as a biblical contemplative. He meditated with one eye on the book and the other on the world. He sat with both. It was a personal form of *lectio divina*. His commentaries on Scripture, perhaps especially the prophets, are witness to this practice.

Hand in hand, it is also safe to say that Dan's contemplative discipline was nourished in his Jesuit formation. To be sure there are plenty of Jesuits for whom silence is just space for the wheels of the mind to spin restlessly and relentlessly forward. But I venture that for Dan it summoned a deep listening. After final vows, his first book was poetry (*Time Without Number*[5]) that testifies to the trajectory of these spiritual disciplines. Poet and contemplative being close, if not perhaps one and the same.

About that time (1958), he wrote to a Catholic Worker under his spiritual direction:

> I recommend to your pursuit at prayer of the implication of the contemplative life. A paradox might say that action is powerless to reveal its own soul, and must turn contemplative to learn what it is (action) or how it seeks justification. St. Therese, and Mother Cabrini wear the same eyes. You could add Edith Stein and Dorothy Day. This means facing life at depth, and preparing, by grace,

4. Forest, ed., "Contemplation," 8.
5. D. Berrigan, *Time*.

life to its mere manifestations, or its counterfeits, or to non-life. Perhaps this too: from the depths of a life of prayer, to judge the relative meanings of witnessing controversy; I do not think the answer is easy or automatic; I only say you will reach a Christian answer . . . [as] one who instinctively chooses in favor of silence, humility, service, the invisible, the person—all. It is obvious to add—and all the spiritual writers love to add it, this is another way of bringing out a big stick against "the world"—that by this we counteract noise, pride, selfishness, etc. What is much richer and hardly understood at all, is 1) the personal growth of an apostle who is also a contemplative is *in the midst of the world*; and 2) the impact in the substratum of grace, of such a [one], on others.[6]

Vocationally, in the midst of the world, Dan might perhaps be called an urban contemplative. His nephew Jerry Berrigan reports him telling that in walking the streets of New York, he encountered the faces of passersby as the beads of a rosary to him, each calling forth a prayer, "a moment to ponder the mysteries each person bore, sorrowful and joyful and glorious mysteries."[7]

This is so in accord with Thomas Merton's mystical experience on the streets of Louisville, that I wonder if he took up the monk's famous vision as a practice of walking meditation. (The vision is so famous that the corner of Fourth and Walnut is bizarrely signed with a historical marker recounting Merton's experience there!) In the center of the shopping district, Merton was all but transported. "I was suddenly overwhelmed with the realization that I loved all those people, that they were mine and I theirs, that we could not be alien to one another even though we were total strangers. It was like waking from a dream of separateness . . ." He almost laughed aloud. "There is no way of telling people that they are all walking around shining like the sun."[8]

Nor is it different in substance or way from Dorothy Day's capacity, rooted in the twenty-fifth chapter of Matthew, of seeing Christ in each face of the prisoner, the hungry, the stranger, the sick. And acting so. Read Dan's accounts of patients in his cancer and AIDS hospice work. Pastor as contemplative.

Still, he sought place for a larger rhythm that included silence and solitude. What became his permanent refuge was a cottage on the bluffs

6. D. Berrigan to Karl Meyer, October 2, 1958, in Martin, "Conversion," 133.

7. J. Berrigan, "Remembering."

8. Merton, *Conjectures*, 18.

of Block Island. It may be that the possibility of such a place first came up when he took hospitality on the Island during his underground sojourn in 1970. In any event, sometime after his prison term, William String-fellow and Anthony Towne arranged for the building of a small cottage across the meadow from their home on land originally connected to the main house. Thereafter, Berrigan made the pilgrimage from New York by train and ferry frequently.

One of the first books Daniel had steered into my hands was *The Wisdom of the Desert*,[9] with an introduction by Thomas Merton recounting how they'd hightailed it for the wilderness when church and empire hooked up. Though heavy weather could blow in, Dan wasn't making so much for wilderness, as a initiating a practice—regularly stepping off mainland "America" for other environs hermitical.

It could indeed be said that Dan was in essence joining a monastic enterprise, if one not highly formalized, for that is how Stringfellow voca-tionally described life together on the Island with Anthony Towne.

> [Anthony's] vocation—as that may be distinguished from his occupation—was, in principle, monastic, as is my own. (That is the explanation of our relationship.) That is, he and I have un-derstood that we had been called to a life of prayer and that the practice of prayer is essentially political—a matter of attention to events and of intercession and advocacy for the needs of hu-man life and of the life of the whole of Creation. Prayer, in this sense, is not pietistic, but, on the contrary, radical involvement in the world as it is prompted in the Word of God. So, coming to the Island to live and work had no connotation of withdrawal or escapism or default for the two of us or either one of us, but, rather, a paradoxical meaning.[10]

Even cloistered on an island, they likewise sought contemplation "in the midst of the world."

Just a note about the cottage itself, (or perhaps more than a few). Bill and Anthony first came to the Island in a community of three. Indeed, though he ended up not staying, the first to arrive was Ray Karras, who taught at the Island School. Before locating and acquiring "the main house," atop the Island's high point, they had envisioned buying land and building. Architectural plans were drawn up for three separate living units connected

---

9. Merton, ed., *Wisdom*.
10. Stringfellow, *Simplicity*, 52.

by passageways to a central common space. But then Ray departed; the house was found, the plans shelved. When preparations began for the Berrigan cottage, the plans suddenly proved handy. An Island contractor was simply handed the ready-made blueprints for one of the living units. It was probably more practicality than conscious design, but Berrigan would reside in one of the original "monastic cells."

Dan was given freedom, walked the land, and chose the spot. Near the cliff, but not too near. The sea was slowly coming for the house. The view was sumptuous and often restful, but real estate was falling into the sea (probably at about the same rate that the Island was growing each year by sand deposit onto the lighthouse beach on the far north end). In fact, Dan's choice of location was not shrewd in the realtor's sense, because a pond behind the cottage wall was draining just underground into the Atlantic, hastening the collapse of that portion of the bluff.

On the other hand, that trickle was perpetually carving a new path, steep and sometimes harrowing to be sure, down to the shoreline. Dan would follow a trail, mown in later years, around the rock wall and dense brush, for his descent to the rocky shoals. He'd return, maybe hauling up a flotsam find, often a lobster-pot buoy broken free on the tide, now to be hung in a row of similar prizes from the railing of the cottage deck.

Let me say I often took that gravel-sliding path myself, more than once in early days with Jim Wallis, and often later with my daughters, Lydia and Lucy, who below would climb the wreckage of a fishing trawler and wade the tide pools in search. So inaccessible, we always had the place entirely to ourselves.

Wild roses flourished thick between the rock wall and the cliff. In season, Dan would harvest rose hips for tea. I was never a fan of the brew. I'm sure it was a healthy drink, more like a tonic, but I forced it down in polite sips and a contemplative half-smile.

Trees were planted in contemplation of memory. The hardiest survivor was a twisted red pine devoted to Paul Mayer's mother, Bertel. Others stayed low to the ground or perished in the assault of winter storms.

Although there was a solid desk just inside, when the weather was right, the deck was Dan's place of choice to write, the Olivetti on a small table overlooking the sea. I wonder how much salt air breathes in certain of his books. An earth flag (depicting the celebrated view from the moon) was raised at the corner over a hammock.

The luxury, this plank porch
like a raft bobbing in the shallows
this million dollar prospect: me
king of the raft, grandly setting down lines
like lifelines to the dead

Sitting, sitting, a broad based Buddha
where life lines converge; or
a camp fire the dead creep toward
to warm their hands.[11]

Forgive me. I, too, loved the place and just describing it seems an act of remembrance and devotion. A sliding glass door provided the view (toward "Portugal, our nearest neighbor on east," as Anthony would say). An expandable dining room table just inside. The interior was finished by Herb Fisher, the Island anarchist and craftsman. He lived very simply and was an inveterate comber of the Island dump, before it was mechanized. Stringfellow told that he would attend gatherings in people's homes, survey the contents, and joke, "Someday this will all be mine." Which is so to explain that desk and cupboards were fashioned of barnwood with handles made from organ stops reading *"basso profundo"* and the like.

The tiny bedroom was itself something of a sanctuary. Like Dan's apartment on 98th Street, the walls were full of photos and art, fitted together closely. A congregation of beloveds.[12] Something parallel prevailed in the bathroom, though in this case the hangings were plaques of awards. This was not organizational put-down. More like keeping applause in its place, a certain self-mockery or a discipline of modesty.

[John Leary:]
"An award for drowning do-gooders," he joked
when honors came his way.[13]

It's important to say that the cottage was a place of hospitality. The expandable table could seat a host of Island friends and guests, Dan's culinary

---

11. D. Berrigan, *Block Island*, 77.

12. When Dan relinquished his claim and the cottage was sold, I was gifted one piece from that wall, a line drawing by Vietnamese artist Vo Dinh of Nhat Chi Mai, a Buddhist nun who immolated herself in 1967 to expose the war.

13. D. Berrigan, of John Leary (+1982+) in *Block Island*, 58.

skills being notorious. In my experience, at the city table his menu ran toward pasta, but on the Island, fish from the oven.

But by hospitality I also mean that he loaned the place out, made it available to others. A calendar in New York kept the schedule. He would drop a note to warn if the summer was filling quickly. His brother, Jerry, and Carol Berrigan were always honored with August. But it was a special offering to those recovering from imprisonment, illness, or contemplating actions. In the early days their names were added to a list at the foot of a poem calligraphed on the wall in his distinctive hand.[14] He once wrote of those guests, that list:

> Then came friends for healing respite
> out of the city's iron clutch
> the desperate amenities
> of Burial Brigade.
> The names kept on the wall
> like a votive wall
> or a litany of linked loves.
> You know them as do I
> by heart: scholars, cooks, poets
> meditators, for whom sea & land
> are one blessing, like the paste
> of spit and dirt, an unguent
> in the Healer's hand.[15]

Jeanie Wylie (now of blessed memory) and I honeymooned there a week in 1984. It was a good, most welcome time, especially since Bill would die the following year, but it must also be said that Jeanie picked up on a certain male ambiance of the monastic environs. She'd felt it from afar and now read it up close—even in the list of mostly male resisters enshrined. She understood and honored the gifts, but her psyche went into, as she put it, "a major state of rebellion." She had a dream in which a woman named Isis rose up in a rage. We had to look it up to confirm our suspicions that the name identified a powerful, even stormy, warrior goddess.[16]

It was also a place in which Berrigan's dreamlife flourished, or so he told Stringfellow.

14. For the poem, see p. 160.
15. Berrigan, *Block Island*, 1.
16. Wylie-Kellermann, *Dying Well*, 28–30.

I've said to Bill uneasily:
dreams in that house are like a hot pot
constantly stirred, fumes intense, voices
grandiloquent. What gives?
Bill paused between beats, like the sea.
Like the sea he's no explainer, but pure depth.
He's not on earth to unravel dreams—
to precipitate them rather, like a slowly turned
vintage vat. Drink, then, and dream on![17]

Guests came for free. In fact, there was a little word of welcome, framed and on a book case, which outlined arrangements. No money was to be exchanged over the place. The digs, like the view, were a gift. If you see some bit of work that needed doing, feel free, but enjoy. My own bit of work, annually attended, was to care for the deck. That usually involved a trip to the lumber yard for a few long boards, some water repellant, and a large borrowed crow bar. Sometimes one board led to another and back to the yard.

One year, while I stayed a longer stretch there on my own, I painted the outside—grey blue stain on cedar shakes. It was serious brushwork, but a delight in the sun and sea breeze; or like the monks say, *ora et labora*. Pray and work. Toward the end of that time Dan arrived and I moved up to the main house, but Bill and I were invited down for dinner that night. After, as drinks continued, Dan produced a check which he passed before me to Bill. The amount, substantial by my lights, seemed either to be what the paint job was deemed worth or simply some amount of Stringfellow's need. He also pulled from a book case and presented to me a clay sculpture of Gandhi's head after a caricature by David Levine. I had to look twice. There was no exchange of money, no *quid pro quo*; it was a sweet and simple circle, entirely of gifts.

The keeper of the keys, though the place was perpetually unlocked, was Jim Reale, town yoga teacher, arborist, and handyperson. He met Dan through Bill, whose right-hand caregiver he'd become for the six months prior to his death. By that route of friendships, Jimmy became first a Plowshares activist and then Berrigan filmmaker. It was under his eye and care that the place was winterized and a new tightly efficient woodstove installed. Hence, Dan's postscript above, concerning winter silence. When

17. Berrigan, *Block Island*, 2.

Bill passed, Jimmy had a hand in the disposition of Stringfellow's library, but that's a story for another time.[18]

The burial of Bill's ashes, side by side with Anthony's disinterred from their place by the flag pole of the main house (now sold) took place a year after the funeral. A group of Island folk, plus friends from across the country, received Dan's hospitality that day. He cooked a feast, but first presided for the simplest of rites, though the *Book of Common Prayer* necessarily had a voice as well. Wallis and I dug the grave. For a marker, a sculpture of Daniel's hands in cuffs flashing the peace sign, rested on the adjacent rock wall. Nightly, the Southlight turned its eye, keeping watch.

18. By Stringfellow's will, the cottage was held until Dan's own death by a trust composed of attorney Ned Hastings, Scott Kennedy, and Jim Wallis.

Film Presence Aside: Saved by Grace from Celebrity

I was shocked, even if moved and delighted, when I first saw a video of the Catonsville Nine action. I assumed such footage did not exist. In a lunch discussion at Union Seminary in 1973 I recall a fellow student arguing that we needed to train ourselves in video technology to capture, preserve, and publicize such actions. A media wonk among us. Personal camcorders were still then a decade off, never mind the ubiquitous video transmitting smart phones of today. I was struck that Dan was wary and then some. He actively discouraged the idea. What developed in my own thinking thereafter was that, especially in actions of prayer and liturgy, cameras stole the center. They were a kind of spiritual intrusion. As a representative power on the scene, they distracted, distorted, inflated, refocused attention, both personal and collective. Moreover, the cults of celebrity are founded upon that temptation, that off-centering, that spiritual inflation. The applause of an audience borne by the pointed lens. (My views, at least about getting the narrative out, have since moderated).

And yet, call it an irony, Daniel Berrigan actually had an important film presence, even a filmography. I propose to run through the latter in shorthand here, but first to comment on the matter of his presence.

Think of Thomas Merton, that celebrated hermit and monk. There are photos of him in monastic life (although the Trappists had a thing about cameras as well).[19] In those that exist, and they tend to be famous ones, he seems to look on, unfazed and guileless—almost childlike, meeting the camera's eye. My feeling is that Dan was similar. If the camera sought to cast its spell, he just let it wash over him, remaining unfazed himself. It's the very reason, bizarre on the face of it, that I set these film reflections in a section on contemplation. He knew how to hold his center under scrutiny. To stay himself. To remain alert and present. To keep things real. Whether by gift or discipline, it shone forth as grace.

I believe filmmaker Roland Joffe saw something of that in him. Dan and the other Plowshares Eight had played themselves in re-enacting their trial for Emile de Antonio's 1983 film *In the King of Prussia*,[20] which also starred fellow activist Martin Sheen as the judge. It was another layer of

19. Fa. Terry Moran is kind to remind me: "Actually there are lots of photos of Merton in monastic life. Under Abbot James Fox, the Trappist became very pro-camera and Fox took every opportunity to publicize Gethsemani in the media. Merton himself wrote the text for a picture book about the monastery though anonymously."

20. de Atonio, dir., *King of Prussia*.

accessible testimony upon the action itself. What I believe caught Joffe's eye was Dan's self-possessed presence. It was like a screen test, not so much about whether he could act, but how he could remain himself, which may be exactly what the movie-maker was after.

Joffe was preparing to make a feature film about the Jesuits in eighteenth-century Paraguay. He phoned to inquire if Dan would be interested in helping and was invited over. The way I heard it from Dan, he opened the door to find Robert DeNiro standing there with the producer, a script in hand. This was going to be a full court press. After some long deliberation, Dan agreed not only to act a character, Fa. Sabastian—Jesuit elder, but to be a consultant to the project.

In general, *The Mission*[21] operates heavily on the level of images, and the story is carried forward on a series of moral decisions. There is the decision of the Jesuits to persevere in their missionary work among the indigenous people of Paraguay after the first attempt ended in martyrdom. With the Guarani peoples of the jungle, they eventually establish a kind of utopian community, rich with a life of music and liturgy, where everything in abundance is held in common and no money changes hands. There is the decision of the papal emissary, arriving poshly arrayed and equipped, to consider the fate of the missions in the light of shifting "new world" geopolitical arrangements between Spain and Portugal. He witnesses firsthand the faith and beauty of what has been created, but bears along the threat of the church in Europe fracturing in disagreement. The lives (and deaths) of the indigenous hang in the balance. Will the missions, which have become both model economic cooperatives (competing successfully with their imperial counterparts) and sanctuary cities of refuge against the Portuguese slave trade, be supported and sanctioned by the Church? Or will the Jesuits be ordered home and the people abandoned, left to a bloody fate or worse?

Beyond that, will the Jesuits comply, bending to a hierarchy for whom authority and control (the issues sound vaguely familiar) outweigh the primacy of gospel demands and options for the poor? They do resist and rightly so, but this only raises the further moral question: by what means? Paths diverge, as two priests, one played by young Liam Neeson, decide for violent resistance. The other is Robert DiNiro's character, Mendoza, a former slave trader and fratricide (whose conversion is poignantly told). He takes up the

21. Joffe, dir., *The Mission*.

sword he once laid down in becoming a Jesuit. Is he, as his mentor and counterpart contends, betraying not only the order, but the gospel?

Here, finally, to a compelling image. The lead Jesuit and mentor, played
by Jeremy Irons, also chooses resistance, though of a different sort, and so
takes his place with the indigenous community gathered in the mission
chapel. As the heavily armed troops approach, having brutally defeated the
armed resistance, the community emerges from the church in liturgical procession. In front, most vulnerable, is the priest bearing the ornate cross mon-
strance, which holds the consecrated host. Together they carry it toward the
soldiers, offering it as the very truth of the moment, and yet another choice.
The soldiers do pause and nearly balk. But military orders prevail and they
fire massively and indiscriminately upon the crowd.

As noted, it was Dan whose consultation turned this final scene from
one of passivity to the more active radical nonviolence and sacramental
resistance. He also appears, mostly in the background, throughout the film,
often in those moments of moral argument and decision-making. He is
there, being himself, with a nod or a wince or a headshake of disbelief. And
once, a single word, "No."

In reflecting on the film and its process, particularly the notable per-
formers, he writes:

> So I record my admiration for the actors' discipline, their endur-
> ance and good temper. Even to a degree, I celebrate their ego, that
> delicate honeycomb of stone, a veritable Great Reef; over it the
> tides of fortune wash and wash. And all in vain.[22]

I would say as much of him, though ego under grace.

For those who linger through the credits to the end (as I am wont to do)
the serial trajectory of decision-making has a final image, a silent one. The
papal nuncio sits at his desk and looks up from his report, eye to eye with
the camera, indeed with ourselves as onlookers and bystanders, suddenly engaged directly. You can see his confession of jaded worldliness and the smug
ethics of necessity, but there is also a question unspoken in his expression:
"Oh yes? And you, what are you doing in your moment of history?"

Just a word further about a central metaphor: the gorgeous and
crushing waterfall that seems to represent the rush of history. Like the
"Sea" of Galilee in Mark's Gospel,[23] the falls are accurately themselves, but

22. D. Berrigan, *Mission*, 85.
23. Myers, *Binding*, 104–5, 114, 150, 230.

also signify. In the opening image, a Jesuit missionary is tied to a cross, sent bobbing down the river, and over into martyrdom. Later in the film, another Jesuit priest and the European soldiers pursuing him in a canoe, likewise suffer its rush and crush. But also, more than one character climbs the rock face beside the torrent, going up to the indigenous community, bare-handed against the force of history.

At the beginning of *Father Daniel Berrigan: The Holy Outlaw,* a documentary by Lee Lockwood about Dan's experience underground, Berrigan stands on a bridge spanning a gorge near Cornell. As the rushing cataract below sings in the background, he reflects:

> Ten years, to the early days of civil rights, my brother Phil was involved in the south in a deep and painful way, and the exchange we were trying to work out in those days was a kind of pre-natal understanding of how north and south might come together without blood, without tragedy, something of course that was never realized. We were beginning to get our own kind of baptism, if I can keep to the image down below here. I think we didn't realize that the waters were apt to turn to blood, that what might happen, has happened. And that old idea of being baptized, reborn might actually cause the death of a very good man. These waters of time have since been dipped in a great deal of blood. From innocent Vietnamese blood, to innocent American blood.[24]

The documentary for NET television includes footage of the Catonsville action, Dan's sermon at Germantown United Methodist Church, an amazing moment of confirmation and blessing by his mother after his arrest, interviews with the Milwaukee Fourteen—a draft board raid which followed, testimony from Howard Zinn, and also interviews with William Stringfellow and Anthony Towne, following their indictment on charges of harboring a fugitive.

Toward the end, in a nod to the old conversation of faithfulness versus effectiveness, Lockwood asks if Berrigan is aware of any indication that his actions have made any difference. Dan replies, "The first evidence of anything really occurring in the lives of others is some evidence that some change has occurred to one's self, and I'm quite certain that that has occurred." The roots of social transformation grow first close to home.

24. Lockwood, dir., *Holy Outlaw.*

Just to say here, Berrigan himself wrote television scripts. During his time teaching at LeMoyne, he wrote screenplays for shows on contemplative Charles de Foucauld, painter Georges Rouault, German Jesuit Rupert Mayer, and Jewish philosopher and concentration camp victim Edith Stein.[25]

His own earliest film appearances were in documentaries about the war. Emile de Antonio's first contact with Berrigan came about from interviewing him, among an array of others, for the 1968 Vietnam War documentary *In the Year of the Pig.*[26] But it was Catonsville that spawned a number of screen events. Dan had turned the legal transcript into a play, *The Trial of the Catonsville Nine,*[27] which was published in the year of his underground sojourn and imprisonment. It premiered at the Lyceum Theatre in New York City in 1971, with an original cast featuring Michael Moriarty, Josef Sommer, Sam Waterston, and James Woods, among others, and has since had a New York revival. Gregory Peck financially backed and produced a 1972 film adaptation starring Ed Flanders as Dan.

In 2001, Lynne Sachs made *Investigation of a Flame,* a documentary about the Catonsville Nine. The forty-five-minute film includes interviews with six of the Nine—Dan and Phil, John Hogan, Thomas Lewis, and married couple Marjorie and Tom Melville. Though interspersed with jangly experimental effects, their reflections two decades after are clear and instructive. In the course of things, Philip makes a striking confession.

> I tended to be too damn angry. I was ashamed of this country and what we were doing in Vietnam and angry as hell over it. While I would never raise a hand to another human being, there was too much contempt in me, too much hatred of the system here, forgetting of course that the system is made up of people. And according to our tradition and religion, according to our scripture, we're obligated to love the people. We're obligated to love even our enemies. And there wasn't much of that in my makeup in those days. At the

---

25. Martin, "Conversion," 150, 159.
26. de Antonio, dir., *Year of the Pig.*
27. D. Berrigan, *Trial.*

same time, I was convinced of the necessity for direct action. And now I know that it is the only resource that people have.[28]

A subsequent Catonsville documentary, *Hit and Stay: A History of Faith and Resistance*,[29] would verify Phil's last claim. This fine feature-length film begins with solid examinations of Catonsville and the Baltimore Four, but its strength is in telling the evolution and history of the action communities that they spawned. Jim Forest has told his surprise that Dan was disappointed the first two had not (yet) led to similar actions—which indeed prompted him into a third, the Milwaukee Fourteen. I confess it was news to me that between 1967 and 1972 there were hundreds of such actions. Moreover, they also evolved, in one direction, toward corporate offices (such as Dow Chemical) or federal agencies (like FBI/Cointelpro) but also toward various creative responses—not just staying to be arrested, but surfacing at a later event, or "taking responsibility" after the fact.

Daniel's time underground is a running backdrop. The film, as a chronicle, does for draft board raids what Artie Laffin has done for Plowshares actions.[30] The voices are many. Along the way there are certain philosophical discussions, including one on celebrity and leadership. Phil's ability to challenge folks and marshal resistance is named. Noam Chomsky comments that it's inevitable, indeed a negative factor, "in a celebrity-run culture that people will be picked out and identified as leaders." Anointed by media for leadership. Others point to a multitude of organizers and warn that mythologizing the Nine (only to touch the hem of their garments) reduces the true call to nonviolent action. The organizing acumen of one John Grady stands out among them. The film lands on a woven telling of two trials—for the Harrisburg Conspiracy and the Camden Twenty-eight draft board raid—both of which involved FBI informants on the stand. The Harrisburg Seven were freed by a hung jury and the Twenty-eight were acquitted by one after the informant turned witness for the defense. As a personal connection, in my seminary days, we put together a student-directed course on the former, and I attended the latter on a day of Dan's testimony. The film ends where my early formation was beginning.

---

28. Sachs, dir., *Investigation of a Flame*.

29. Tropea and Cyzyk, dirs., *Hit and Stay*.

30. Laffin, *Plowshares*.

By my lights (and I have reason to be biased), two of the best documentaries are the most recent. Both are collaborative efforts between Sue Hagadorn and the Reale brothers. The first, *Seeking Shelter: A Story of Faith, Place, and Resistance,*[31] is, on the one hand, a love letter to Block Island (where the Reales and even Sue have some personal footing) and on the other, an account of Dan's underground sojourn that was ended at the home of his dear friends there, Stringfellow and Towne. The thirty-minute short includes observations about the latter's influence on the political culture of the Island and its environmental protection against overdevelopment. It's framed by Stringfellow himself reading aloud from his most beautifully written book, *A Simplicity of Faith: My Experience in Mourning.*[32] The film was made with loving help and support from Bill's friends on the Island, as was an accompanying exhibit that sometimes travels with the film.[33]

It's fair to call the second one, *The Berrigans, Devout and Dangerous,*[34] a family film—for a variety of reasons. The Reale brothers are again on screen and soundtrack. Before the title even appears, Frida Berrigan sets the stage, introducing her Mom and Dad and her Uncle Dan. Of Liz and Phil, over a series of stills, "Lucky for me they found one another; they fell in love; they got married; they were excommunicated. And they had children—me, my brother Jerry, and our sister Kate." On notice: we are opening a family album. Each photo will have a story, personal and intimate. Can a camera lens admit love?

Shortly and with a slight chuckle, Dan reports phoning his mother to say he's out of jail for his Pentagon first arrest, but that Phil has been taken. "She said, 'Let me get this straight; you're out and he's in?' and I said yeah." Later in the film, a television media reporter presses her about the morality of the Catonsville action. Does she support them in breaking the law? A thoughtful pause, then firm, "Yes I do, because it's not God's law."

This is not the first attempt to tell the story of both brothers together. The film's title is an echo of an earlier double biography, *Disarmed and*

---

31. Hagadorn, dir., *Seeking Shelter.*

32. Stringfellow, *Simplicity.*

33. *Seeking Shelter: The Exhibition,* https://www.seekingshelterblockisland.org/seeking -shelter-the-exhibition.html.

34. Hagadorn et al., dirs., *Devout and Dangerous.*

Dangerous.[35] There really is no one-without-the-other. Phil, pushing Dan into direct action, knew he was also saving him from career—a comfortable Ivy League niche, "going for tenure, living out his life in genteel wine and cheese obscurity."

Yet Dan could also save Phil from himself, from deadly seriousness. Late in the film Frida tells of how the three brothers would gather in Syracuse. She could see them begin to let down with one another, telling jokes, spinning stories, letting out with a great rolling belly guffaw which she could replicate, and does—delighting to see her father so. Dan's humor comes through repeatedly—his impish grin—telling of his underground escape, appearing on the *Dick Cavett Show*, or flummoxing a reporter outside the courthouse.

Initially, the focus of this project was Dan alone. I have seen a nearly completed take of the preliminary version. It included more overlap with the Block Island short, and if I may say, somewhere in the can is a very good film about Daniel Berrigan. But adding Elizabeth, Philip, and clan was genius, even if it meant acquiring additional footage. Greatly done.

The big events, like Catonsville, Harrisburg, and the Plowshares Eight, are closely covered. Classic footage is there along with the new and obscure. Dan's underground excursion is begun, for example, with a whisper in the ear and a moving procession of Bread and Puppet effigies—which were his vehicle of escape. The effect of all these is measured personally with political consequence. I have heard other versions of Daniel Ellsberg's ethical impetus for releasing the Pentagon papers (Franz Jagerstatter's witness or Norman Morrison's self-immolation outside the Pentagon), but here he attributes the draft board raid.

Narrative threads are provided by the voices of friends and family: Jeremy Scahill—a Catholic Worker and journalist who founded *The Intercept*, Jim Forest—Dan's friend and recent biographer, Martin Sheen—actor and civil disobedient, Jerry Berrigan—brother, and Frida—daughter, niece, and movement activist. Most often the narrative is carried by the voices of Liz, Phil, and Dan themselves. Full disclosure of my bias: I was interviewed for the film and also provided footage, archival and original.

Where passages of Daniel's poetry are included, they are voiced by Liam Neeson, and illustrated by a dream-like technique of animated brush strokes over moving images. Stunning.

---

35. Polner and O'Grady, *Disarmed and Dangerous*.

Brother Jerry's storytelling of their Minnesota family life is touching, both for the goodness their mother imparted, but also the unpredictable volatility of the father—of which Dan as a frail kid got the brunt. So it was all the more touching to hear him tell of Dan's close accompaniment and even mutual forgiveness in Pop's last days.

Set beside that Phil's son, named for his Uncle Jerry, sitting at his father's bedside for dying time conversation. He speaks of the rhythm of his breathing, slowing to match his dad's. Jerry had brought along tools from Michigan in hopes of building a wheel-chair ramp for walks, but Phil "cuts to the chase," realistic about his time, and asks him to build a coffin. I was blessed to be among friends who followed in procession behind that casket on a pick-up bed. To see the images of that crowd, Dan treading among us, is practically sacramental. Like the scene, outside Jonah House, of Liz leading us as cinematic visitors to Philip's grave and headstone.

In the middle of things, Jeremy Scahill makes the point:

> How do we live our lives if we're going to live lives of resistance? How are you going to confront the big lie that the only way of structuring our life is the nuclear family? And that's kind of how you have the origin of Jonah House. The idea of Jonah House is that everyone is in community together; they're growing together; raising children together; resisting together; they're working together. You broaden the definition of family much wider.

I couldn't agree more, and it is verily a point of the film. But I would quickly add: that marriage, that Berrigan family was the anchor and heartbeat of Jonah. It was the constant. It was the center that held things together for decades. Everyone else was welcomed in as community, deeply held, and at some point moved on to the work in another place.

At one point, under journalistic pressure, almost harassment, about their action, Dan rejoins, "We're not trying to play God. We're trying to play human." Humanity, human family, in exquisite and clumsy fullness, is the sweet theme here. This is not to take the edge off their risks and consequences, but to put on them flesh, relationship, spirit, and tenderness. Thanks be.

— Chapter 11 —

Inspiration: A Voice in Discernment

I dunno if this helps. It helps me just to peck it out, however clumsily. I know, as always, your own reflection will be an immense help to us all. So will the action. Because it proceeds from "the deep heart's core." (Yeats) Happy Easter, Daniel[1]

To be honest, much of what I know about spiritual and vocational discernment I've learned from the process of planning nonviolent, liturgical, direct actions of civil resistance.[2] But also, in both regards, from Daniel Berrigan. Let me tell a personal story, not altogether self-flattering, to frame some observations.

In 1982 a group of us who had already been engaging in anti-nuclear resistance came together: Fa. Bob Bossie, Br. Jerry Ebner, Fa. Gordon Judd, Fa. Tom Lumpkin, Fa. Larry Rosebaugh, Maria West, and myself. Just two years prior, the first "Plowshares action" had taken place when Daniel along with his brother and six other friends[3] entered a General Electric plant in Pennsylvania and used blood and hammers to damage or "convert" a Mark 12A nuclear warhead. Their deed, enacting Isaiah's call to beat swords into plowshares, had sparked a movement—and we were prepared to consider if and how we might join it.

We began a year-long series of monthly weekend retreats in different locations around the Midwest to contemplate a time and place to act. Those retreats consisted of prayer, Bible study, community building, and reading the signs of the times—each of which offered opportunity to "listen for the Word."

---

1. D. Berrigan to Wylie-Kellermann, March 14, 1982, author's files.

2. Adapted from Wylie-Kellermann, "Eucharist at Gunpoint."

3. Philip Berrigan, Carl Cabot, Dean Hammer, Elmer Maas, Anne Montgomery, Molly Rush, and John Schuchardt.

Intercession as discernment? Yes. For whom are we praying and so, by extension, for whom and where and how are we to act? Eventually, we would make an "altar cloth" to be used in the action liturgy, writing upon it the names of individuals and communities, even nations, on whose behalf we acted.

With this moveable retreat—Wisconsin, central Illinois, Michigan— each locale enabled us to meet close to a military base or weapons manufacturing facility. There was a practical matter of scoping out prospects and reconnoitering the landscape, but that joined with a spiritual task of listening. Were our hearts pulled to this place?

Reading together the signs of the times influenced our sense of location. In brief, at that moment the cruise missile, a versatile first-strike weapon, was being forward-based in Europe, and the Women of Greenham Common were engaging a campaign of intransigent resistance, an ongoing encampment. Meanwhile, the cruise was just then being mounted on B-52s at Wurtsmith AFB in northern Michigan, rendering an otherwise "deterrent weapon" first-strike capable. So the times commended a place.

As a gift of the Spirit, I comprehend discernment to be essentially communal—not only best undertaken in community, but for its wider sake. In our community-building work, for example, we made confession to one another, including confessing our fears. When fears are secreted and silenced, they hold us back. Yet often as not, the very things we fear are precisely what we're called to do. Kept inside they rule us, working in the service of the powers. Confessed into the light of community they can be freed to be in the service of the Spirit.

Conscience, call it a charismatic gift, may indeed be found in solitary witness and discernment. I am thinking here of the life and conviction of Franz Jagerstatter, Austrian war resister to Nazism, but it's certainly best nourished and tested in communal spirituality.[4]

Naming fears necessarily points to the principalities and powers with whom we struggle. The Law, as such, is among them. The power of death, primarily in the form of imprisonment, but even execution, stands behind its dictates. To break the law conscientiously entails discerning its spirit, and facing the threat. In a Birmingham jail cell, Martin Luther King, Jr. struggled to articulate this discernment. How do we distinguish, say, between a just law that merits our obedience and an unjust law that

---

4. For a while, Dan had a full-sized wood carving of Jagerstatter in his 98th St. apartment.

conscience requires be broken? How do we recognize when a law, otherwise just on the face of it, is being applied unjustly? In our case, how does the law enable and protect nuclear devastation? Is the law serving community and creation, or siding with their destruction?

In these retreats, Bible study figured into this very process. We had, of course, attended to Isaiah 2 and the beating of swords into plowshares. But as the liturgical year turned before us, we began to read together some of the Easter lections—and here came a remarkable discovery. After the crucifixion of Jesus, by Matthew's account (27:62f.), the religious authorities remember what the disciples have so quickly forgotten: the promise of resurrection. They suffer a great anxiety that, by one means or another, he might not stay put, and so they appeal to the governor. Pilate, in response, provides a guard of soldiers and "makes the sepulcher secure by sealing the stone." This seal is a legal matter. Cords would be drawn across the stone and anchored with clay. As explicit in the book of Daniel (6:18) the clay would be impressed with an official signet—the empire's own? To move the stone would indicate tampering. To break the official seal would be a civil offense. Resurrection is against the law. Or so we discerned in our reading together.

I have a vivid memory of the moment when Tom Lumpkin of the Detroit Catholic Worker said, "What I would like to do is celebrate the Easter Vigil Liturgy, walking onto the base toward the loaded B-52s." There was almost an audible thump in my own chest, one I swear could be heard in others around the circle. We all knew a plan was set.[5]

When the pre-dawn moment came, we lit the paschal candle and formally cut the barbed wire fence, breaking the seal of legal security, and so proclaiming resurrection freedom from the power of death. But first there was another discernment to endure. We had resolved, and would eventually succeed, in walking several miles of runway to the open gates of the deadly-force high-security area filled with cruise-missile-armed B-52s. Is this a place, I now asked, we want to begin swinging hammers? Over several weeks, a heavy debate ensued among us.

To join the conversation, Dean Hammer and Philip, both from the original King of Prussia Plowshares, joined us for a day-long retreat with Bible study, taking us back to Isaiah 2. I needed no convincing on the wisdom, urgency, and nonviolence of Plowshares actions, but the questions became: is

---

5. For another description of the action see, Wylie-Kellermann, *Seasons*, xix–xxiv.

this the place to let fall the hammer? in a deadly force zone is it an invitation to violence? did we need to drop the tool or shift the location?

I wrote a letter to Dan. Then, by chance on a visit to Gethsemani Abbey to pray over things, I ran into John Schuchardt, likewise from the original action. Providence granted a walk and a talk with him in those Kentucky hills. He asked good questions. When Dan wrote back he began somewhat Zen in fashion, as in read-your-own-heart-in-these-lines, but then actually came down in line with my concerns:

> I donno about all this. On the one hand, I wasn't part of a long trail of obscurity to mabbe to let's go. That's a limitation which is almost a predicament. On the other, I know you, Dean and Phil about as well as I know anyone in the "wale" of tears as Mrs. Gummidge puts it mournfully. Therefore what follows.
>
> (I know our exchange will be betwixt us two, as well). I guess it could be sed, Phil peddles hardware, I peddly software. There's also some difference discernable in the power of symbols vs. literal damages. I agree with all my heart that the best thing we can do in such places as you describe, is to celebrate eucharist—as long as there is accompanying c.d. of some sort. This latter (as 2 tactics) is relatively indifferent to me. Its enuf to say; I prayed where prayer was forbidden because death is in charge.
>
> On the west coast there is some discomfiture on score of eastern insistence on symbols + damage. I like I guess to call the thing one; symbolic damage; but the one ought to keep the two in balance, some damage through symbols. I think the eucharist supplies the balance; the broken bread sez we break death's stranglehold—ultimately being willing to be broken, by being where we are, doing what we do. And so the wine; about life being precious certainly, but here freely given, not wasted. WHATEVER follows on this I consider secondary, in the sense that the main act has been done; Even while I think some thoughtful follow through is also required—to bring the eucharist to bear, so to speak.
>
> I might as well say it, hammers appear to me in such circumstance as you describe, just too flatfooted, literal, a kind of alternative weapon to the nukes themselves, and therefore exciting the worst in the death urges of those guarding . . . Hammers lose the balance, for me. I don't think you're in there to dare them to use guns on you because you've used hammers on their dears. (In K.o.P[6] there was no such dare, it was all freakishly free & easy . . .)[7]

---

6. King of Prussia, Pennsylvania.

7. D. Berrigan to Wylie-Kellermann, March 14, 1982. I note that the Kings Bay

Need I say the letter was a gift to me, clarifying and crystalizing my own thoughts? It was also a potential gift to movement and community, but not one I was free to readily circulate or share. It seemed I could only honor it by being more firm.

Fa. Larry Rosebaugh, OMI, one of the truly great souls among us, a veteran of conscientious action, including federal time for simply trespassing and praying in a nuclear weapons plant, made a final attempt. He hand-carved a hammer, more akin to a heavy wooden meat tenderizer, after the fashion of an indigenous tool. Could we carry it along with the intent of beating the nuclear swords to plowshares? Was even the intent reckless? Would it come into play? My firmness became intractable. No supple listening heart, almost rigid in righteousness. I wonder now, and here confess, that I may have blocked genuine discernment. Thwarting, perhaps, the Holy Spirit herself.

This to say that spiritual and political discernment is not a tidy process. Actually, quite messy—listening for the divine in the stuff of the human. Its community dimension, even its many voices, is so crucial precisely because it can be fraught with ego or worse. In the end you just have to trust it to God and together do the deed.

Our action turned out true and beautiful. The Spirit did not abandon us. Halfway down the runway we renewed our baptismal vows, looking toward the bombers while "renouncing Satan and all his works." At the open gate of the high security area, we spread the intercessory altar cloth, scattered vials of our own blood in the name of the Lamb, and partook of Eucharist at gunpoint surrounded by military vehicles. Outside, at churches and the front gatehouse, friends distributed our leaflet:

> We believe that God has already intervened in this dark history of ours.
>
> We believe there is hope. Many people have yielded to despair. They can already hear the terrible sound of the door slamming shut on human history. But we are here to say otherwise. Someone is hidden at the heart of things, breaking in to break out, on behalf of human life.
>
> We believe that God rules our common history. Not the Soviet Union. Not the United States. Not the NATO or Warsaw Pact forces. Despite their big and competing claims.

Plowshares seem to have had a similar discussion, divvying up tools and locations, and not carrying hammers into the deadly force area.

We believe that human beings (so says Easter), are free from the power of death in all its forms and delivery systems. We are not stuck with the balance of terror arrangements. We're not in bondage to these weapons. We are truly and fully free to unmake them. Now. Not tomorrow or next week or next year. But this very morning.

We believe that God who raised Christ from the dead will also quicken our imaginations, and thereby our bodies and lives.

We believe this is the meaning of the resurrection. And we've come to say so.[8]

Or so we had discerned. Thanks be to God.

8. Wylie-Kellermann, *Seasons*, xxiii.

Inspirational Aside: Words Can't Make It Happen

Good Evening.[9] Thank you to Satori Shakuur and to all the storytellers of the evening.

The last time that I tried to cross into Canada I was stopped at the border. After a few questions I was sent to a waiting area, and the wait was long. Eventually a woman came to the plexiglass window and she had one of those thick folded computer printouts. "Have you ever been arrested?" she said. "Yeah." She leaned forward and said, "Tell me about depredation of property in Alexandria Virginia in 1979." "I'm pretty sure it was the anniversary of the bombing of Hiroshima, and we poured blood on the pillars of the Pentagon and used our bodies to lock the doors shut as a protest against US nuclear policy."

She looked down the list, shaking her head. I knew it was my rap sheet [laughter], but more what I'd actually like to think of as a history of conscience. I wondered what all was there. I knew it was not just Pentagon but there could be the White House, the Capitol, assorted SAC Bases, missile factories, the federal buildings here in Detroit, and the Detroit Economic Club. [Laughter.] One time I was arrested for dumpster-diving food for a soup kitchen in Grand Rapids. And I actually fell in love with my wife Jeannie when we were handcuffed together [laughter] repeatedly, [laughter] coming and going from the Oakland County jail. We were charged with contempt and conspiracy under the prosecutorial regime of L. Brooks Patterson in those days.

My first arrest was as a seminarian in New York City, at a Columbia University military think tank. I had fallen under the sway of Daniel Berrigan. Berrigan is a Jesuit Priest, a poet, a prophet of nonviolence. And he came to teach at the seminary fresh from two years in federal prison for burning draft files in Catonsville, Maryland as a protest against the war in Southeast Asia. Berrigan knocked me off my horse. Here I was, raised in the church, already in seminary, and suddenly I'm going through a conversion to the gospel. It was his life of course, but concretely the way that he read Scripture, not just as a poet, though that for sure, but as if it was a matter of life and death. He followed a Jesus who was executed for resistance to the official violence of occupation and empire, and now I was following too.

Actually I think the seed of this call went back further, because one time, rummaging through my attic, I stumbled on my high school term

9. Wylie-Kellermann, "Words Can't Make it Happen."

paper, where you learned in those days to use note cards for footnotes. And my paper was on civil disobedience. I was actually shocked to remember it. So, Gandhi, and Thoreau, but especially Martin Luther King's Letter from a Birmingham Jail where he explains the importance of direct action and civil disobedience in the Freedom Struggle.

I graduated from Cooley High School in 1967. I know that that letter affected how I saw the smoke rising from Twelfth Street corridor that summer, the fires of the Detroit Rebellion. There's a passage, I won't quote it accurately, but Dr. King is accused of bringing violence to the city and he says "we didn't bring violence to Birmingham, violence was here. We just brought it into the open, into the light of day."

Perhaps you know that last year was the fiftieth anniversary of that Letter, and on the very date, April 16, the Detroit City Council voted on the Jones Day contract. Now, Jones Day, as I trust you are aware, is the third largest law firm in the world with their main clients being the very banks that have eaten the substance out of our neighborhoods with predatory mortgages. Yes, the same banks who have made predatory loans to the city of Detroit, the so-called Swaps and Cops. It's the law firm partnered by Emergency Manager Kevyn Orr. As of this week, Detroit's been under emergency management for one year. Can you believe that virtually every African American city in the state of Michigan, half the state's African American population, live under non-elected governments? Three-quarters of our black elected officials have been replaced by emergency managers.

So when the Jones Day contract came up for a vote before City Council, I kinda knew this was an important moment. A group of us, mostly young people actually, went to City Council that morning. We spoke during the public comment period. My own comments concerned the anniversary of the Letter and how it's addressed to white pastors. Dr. King expresses great disappointment at the tepid passivity of white pastors in the Freedom Struggle and, to be honest, that had laid a claim on me.

So, when the moment came for the vote, this whole group of us knelt down in the aisle and we began to sing "We shall not, we shall not be moved. We shall not, we shall not be moved. Just like a tree that's planted by the water, we shall not be moved." When we did that, several things happened. One was that it seemed to release and free the whole crowd who was there, maybe sixty or eighty people, present to speak on this issue and others. They all rose up simultaneously and started addressing the council directly. To be frank, there was a lot of anger in the room. I remember one man pounding his hand on the rail in front of the Council area. There was a Korean War veteran who pleaded with the Council, saying, "I fought for this country for four years and now they're going to take my house away in foreclosure." Lots of anger and chaos. So we would sing slowly and loudly trying to bring the focus back down. One woman, gorgeously dressed with this wide brimmed Sunday morning hat, was there to talk about her mother's water bill. She came and stood with us; she had the voice of an angel and when she joined us, suddenly we sounded like we were a choir [laughter], with harmony and rhythm.

Well, we expected that we would be arrested pretty quickly, but in fact we sang for an hour and a half. We could see the police arrive. Actually, officers came pretty quickly, visible through the glass doors. They had handcuffs ready to go. Most of the Council had left the room and some of them appeared with the police, clearly urging arrest. On the other hand there were two Council members, Councilwomen JoAnn Watson and Brenda Jones, who stayed right in their seats. I believe they remained to witness what was happening and receive it, but also to protect us with their presence. So the police were put in this conflict, first of all in themselves. On the one hand they were under orders, and on the other, it was their pensions put up for grabs at the hands of Jones Day. And they knew that; they knew that.

Something else happened that I've never experienced before: someone I know a little bit began whispering in my ear. "Reverend, you've done what you came to do. It's, you know, time to stop." And I said, "No, we're not stopping." And he came back a minute later, the voice whispering in my ear urging "Reverend Charles Williams," who I do know, and trust, and work with, "he wants you to stop, he thinks you should stop." I doubted that was true, but I said "We're not stoppin." And the voice came one more time, saying "Look, we have the votes to prevent this thing; we need to let them vote." That was not true; that proved not to be true. And it was also an untruth that was now being spread through the crowd. I confess I've had voices like that in my own head before. You know, don't do this, or you've taken it far enough, you know, back off, step back. But I've never had this literal whispering in my ear. I think about how the media in Detroit are whispering all the time in our ears saying, "This is just the way it is, and there's nothing you can do about it. Stand down."

Well, eventually when the officers did come in, the woman with the broad Sunday hat, bless her soul, she was with us ready to go—she held out her hands to be cuffed. So did the Korean War vet—offered himself as part of this. But in the end only two of us were arrested: myself and Elena Herrada, a member of the elected Detroit School Board, a warrior in the struggle for children and justice in the city. We were handcuffed and taken through the crowd, down the elevator, to Jefferson where a big blue police bus waited. And immediately, we went to the back of the bus thinking, Oh there were going to be more waves of arrests and this thing is going to fill up. But no. It wasn't long and the bus pulled out. We had the entire thing to ourselves going to the precinct [laughter]—where we were congenially processed. And I should say that when we were released into our own recognizance that the police officers thanked us, and one even embraced us.

In the months that followed we had a number of times in thirty-sixth district court. At the arraignment we requested a jury trial. And the judge said, "Why do you want a jury trial for petty misdemeanor?" and we answered, "Because under emergency management, a jury is the last vestige of official democracy in the city of Detroit." And that's true. We were defending ourselves; we didn't want lawyers. The judge and the prosecutor, and any number of people would repeatedly say to us when we told we were defending ourselves—they would quote the adage, "a lawyer who would defend himself or herself has a fool for a client," The implication, of course, was that we had fools for lawyers [laughter]. But we knew that we would be able to speak more freely, and we wanted to put ourselves on the stand. Our idea was to put Jones Day on trial. And we were set with a number of witnesses, including the honorable JoAnn Watson, prepared to testify who could say she was there and could testify to what happened but she would also be an expert witness on the state of Detroit, on the conflict of interest involved, and the legal malfeasance implied in the contract. On the day of the trial, I was all prepared, thinking if we got to the end of the trial, what I would say to the jury in my closing statement. And because juries are instructed: you can consider this but you can't consider this, you know. And of course what they can't consider is conscience, their conscience and ours, the context for action and what's going on in the city. I was trying to think of how I could let them know the power that they actually have. Because in the end they just say "guilty" or "not guilty." They have way more power than they're allowed to know. And that's what it comes down to being that last vestige of democracy.

Well, on the morning of the trial, the police officers didn't show up. And they were the prosecution's whole case. I don't know, was it the weather, the polar vortex? [laughter]. Did they make a decision; did they think they were giving us a gift? In any event, by their not being present the judge dismissed the charges against us, and we never got to say what we did or why we did it, which I suppose, is why I'm telling you [laughter]. Maybe story listeners are the last vestige of democracy in Detroit.

["Not guilty!"—from the audience] Conscience prevails [laughter].

Next week, I'm going to New York City just for a day or two, I want to see Daniel Berrigan. He's ninety-three. His mind is really sharp but his body is quite frail. I want to thank him, not only for the fifty-some books he's written that've moved my soul, but for the quality of his life and his witness of action over and over and over.

Maybe I'll end with a poem of his. He's a brilliant poet. So, this is something just short:

> For every 10,000 words
> there's a deed
> floating somewhere
> head down, unborn
>
> Words can't make it happen
> They only wave it away
> unwanted.
> Yet Child, necessary one
> Unless you come home to my hands
> Why hands at all?
> Your season your cries
> are their skill
> their reason.[10]

Thank you.

---

10. I only know this poem from a poster, "Honoring Daniel Berrigan at Seattle University 1992," and as an invocation/admonition to Myers, *Binding*.

— Chapter 12 —

A Life Unchained: Dying and Rising

I ONCE HAD A conversation with Dan about his death.[1] We were talking late into the night at the Block Island hermitage that William Stringfellow and Anthony Towne had built for him after he was two years in Danbury Federal Prison in consequence of the Catonsville draft board action. He had by then foresworn scotch, on doctor's orders, so I was being introduced to Manhattans dry, which were somehow allowed. The place was fitting for the topic. On the wall above us was an exorcism poem that he had hand-lettered on the wall in a style familiar to Worker and resistance houses across the country.

At landsend
where this house dares stand
and the sea turns in sleep
ponderous, menacing
and our spirits fail and run
landward, seaward, askelter,
+
we pray you protect
from the law's clawed reach
from the second death
from envy's tooth
from doom's great knell
all who dwell here.[2]

1. Adapted from Wylie-Kellermann, "Death Shall Have No Dominion."
2. I don't believe he ever published this apart from the handwriting on the wall. I have it here from my own journal.

I'm certain I was the one to broach the topic of death. When we met in my seminary days in the early '70s, it was in the wake of notorious assassinations: Medgar Evers and Viola Liuzzo, Fred Hampton and the Panthers. There was a certain youthful grandiosity in imagining that he or Phil or others who were such troublesome peacemakers would be similarly targeted. I braced my heart. I told him so. (Then he turns around and lives, thanks be to God, to age ninety-four!)

(Just pertinent parenthesis, at Dan's seventy-fifth birthday party in New York, Jeanie and I sat next to Jim Douglass for a bit. Across the long table was Howard Zinn, and Douglass was lobbying him hard to write a book connecting the assassinations of Malcom, King, John and Robert Kennedy. He was making such a good and detailed case that Zinn eventually turned it back on him, "No. You should write it!" And Douglass has since produced momentous pieces in a series.)[3]

On the Island with Dan, I probably mentioned King myself, and Bonhoeffer, the way the blood of the martyrs is seed of movement or church, even yearning secretly myself for some sort of "meaningful death." He gently countered with Albert Camus's good life and the absurdly random car crash of his death. So, I was as much chastened as honored when he turned the conversation into a Block Island poem:

> Drinking one night, Kellermann and I
> talked the moon down, 'Think of mad racers
> we're at the mercy of
> And stuttering engines of air craft
> so high the guardian angels peel away—
> Then street knifings. And bloody so on.
> It's certain we exist
> courtesy of bellicose junkers, by merest
> suffrance.'
> Significant death?
> Gold leaf of history, cosmetic
> on a split skull.[4]

---

3. See Douglass, *JFK*; Douglass, *Gandhi*; Douglass, "The Converging Martyrdom of Malcolm and Martin." "The Unspeakable" is a term Thomas Merton coined to name evil of a depth that goes beyond the capacity of words to convey.

4. Berrigan, *Block Island*, 67.

There is sure and certain modesty in that. Worth being chastened by. But he could also quip that if you wanted to follow Jesus, "you better look good on wood." Didn't discipleship summon us into the passion? In fact, he could lament the lack.

> That passion shaped us. But then we cooled. People once died for beliefs (killed others too). But we come swaddled in something called security, dogma, from cradle clothes to shroud. And who today dies for anything at all, anyone at all? We don't die "for"; we die "of"; decline and fall. The martyr is now the patient.[5]

There is the story of Dan almost dying while imprisoned at Danbury. He had been given a shot of Novocain for some dental work to be done and the procedure went south, an allergic reaction that sent him into shock. Prison or not, it would have been an absurd sort of death, about which he is utterly candid in his description.

> It was like being on a high, like "going up." You know the old paintings? One just sort of hovered above everybody, you know? It wasn't particularly unpleasant, except that I was a little cha-grinned. I thought a dirty trick was being played on me. I hadn't been told the rules of the game, and suddenly they were being ap-plied. I mean, to die from a shot of Novocain is a very absurd thing when you think you should go out big.[6]

On Block Island, three days before his capture by the FBI at Stringfel-low's home, he recorded a message to the Weather Underground, subse-quently published in *The Village Voice*. It reflected a realism about his own situation and the risks under which he lived.

> And this is why we accept trouble, ostracism, and fear of jail and of death as the normal condition under which decent men and women are called upon to function today. Undoubtedly, the FBI comes with guns in pursuit of people like me because beyond their personal chagrin and corporate machismo (a kind of debased es-prit de corps; they always get their man), there was the threat that the Panthers and the Vietnamese have so valiantly offered. The threat is a simple one; we are making connections . . .[7]

---

5. D. Berrigan, *Ten Commandments*, 145.

6. D. Berrigan, *Absurd Convictions*, 97.

7. D. Berrigan, *America*, 92–93.

Our last conversation, some months before his death, was partly about Dietrich Bonhoeffer again. The new Charles Marsh biography, so honest and revealing, was out. He'd not heard tell.

It was actually on the twenty-fifth anniversary of Bonhoeffer's death by hanging in the Nazi prison of Flossenberg that Berrigan went underground in 1970. That day he began a long poetic review of Eberhard Bethge's elephantine Bonhoeffer biography just then out, publishing it in *Saturday Review*. Such publication was maddening to FBI director J. Edgar Hoover. Like other initiatives, popping up to preach in a prominent pulpit or appearing on network television and then skipping out the back door, it improvised a nation of safe houses and kept Berrigan on the Most Wanted List.

Acknowledging the footnoted churchy stuff, Berrigan honed on the distillate.

> "Bonhoeffer: *I am working with all my might for church resistance. But it is perfectly clear to me that this resistance is only a temporary and transitional phase that will lead on to opposition of a quite different kind. . . . [P]ray with us that it will be a 'resistance unto death,' and that people will be found to suffer it."*

> Berrigan: *"To the question of whether the church should connive with the state in the suppression, deportation, and murder of Jews, he proposed a concrete answer: the formation at Finkenwalde, in 1936, of a [community] of young seminarians, to engage in study, discipline, and prayer, and (in the event, only known afterward) to prepare of resistance and death."*

This too was a topic that Dan and William Stringfellow were discussing in those last few underground days. Could such a seminary take form on US soil in a different moment? Though they took this up again in earnest after Berrigan's release from prison, it would be wrong to think imprisonment was an interruption of some sort. It was, in fact, the immediate tryout behind bars. Pulling together that circle of draft resisters and conventional felons, Dan convened the group for study, discipline, and prayer, which eventually busted out upon the world. And only then would a group of us at Union Seminary be drawn into its next iteration.

I think again here of Dan's *Letter to the Vietnamese*. Even now, I can look up and see it on my wall as a series of connected posters with art by Tom Lewis.

A universal malevolent will, crouched like a demon
blows winter upon us, stiffens our limbs in death, the limbs of
women and children.
Here, they hawk death in the streets, death in the hamburg joint
death in the hardware, death in the cobbler's hammer
death in the jeweler's glass, the classy showrooms of death.
Death, shouts the newsboy; death, oranges and lemons,
death in a candy wrapper.
Death, the cinema blares it; death![8]

He did write in winter, bitterly cold, and one can feel the toll on his lifelong ailments of bone and back and limb. But each ache is a reminder, a connection, an intercession. As he concludes, "It is snowing tonight as I vigil, the first white fall of winter. I think on the fevers and horrors of Con Son. No to their No. Yes to all else."

Death, the great No with a capital N, is everywhere in the culture, riddling it all. How does one say No and also Yes? One way, of course, is the invention of liturgical direct action and its consequences. Ritually damaging nuclear warheads in such as the Plowshares actions or, before that, the draft board raids like Catonsville, burning the files with homemade napalm.

But side by side with these, Dan was tending the dying. Like Camus's doctor in *The Plague*, he tended victims while saying No to the executioners. In the '80s he sat to the end with AIDS patients, the untouchables ravaged by both disease and culture. I have notes from him on cards depicting Christ crucified by AIDS. In *Sorrow Built a Bridge*, he recounted, eyes wide open with love, their crossings over.

Earlier, he had done the same at a hospice for the dying in Manhattan—specifically, the dying poor with cancer. Needless to say, he made the connections—they were woven whole cloth into his life. He recognized Hiroshima as the emblem of unleashed fallout in culture, history, planet. Genes corrupted by the radioactive poisoning of water and air were simply to be seen as the ailment of this world. Cancer? They declare war on that, too. The targeting of civilians in the atomic bombing flowed from the long-time casting off and casting out of the poor. All one before the war god Mars.

Berrigan also told their stories. *We Die Before We Live* reads partly like a journal, feeling his way forward in the hospice halls, learning the clumsy

8. See above, pp. 172–77.

arts of touch or silence or a word, even prayer. But largely the book collects vignettes, accounts of the dying, their ways and faces.

Dan had been led to the hospice by a young Catholic Worker serving there as an orderly. I suggest the influence of the Worker here in a further way. Going back to the days of Dorothy, the New York paper had a practice, picked up by others around the country, of eulogizing guests who would ordinarily cross over in the silence of blank and nameless obscurity.[9] Often as not, sizing up characters fit for a Dickens novel, these descriptions could be funny and heroic and quirky, but above all honest and loving. I always read them. And I know the style crept into my own approach to doing funeral liturgies.

If you find the gospel in someone's story only by smoothing the facts, then it's really less than the gospel and actually less than truly human as well. Consider how much of conventional burial liturgy is taken up with smoothing and fluffing as denial. Or saying carefully, in effect, nothing at all. Face-painting a corpse. Anyway, thanks be for the humor, poignancy, and refusal to look away evinced by those tales.

In 1985 Berrigan preached Stringfellow's eulogy on Block Island. Beside a culture of betrayal, political, economic, spiritual, in the nation and on the Island, he set Bill as a non-betrayer, a keeper of his word, indeed the Word of God. He declared:

> A sophisticated people is struck by a shortage of words adequate to describe a bad time and how one might meet it. So we grope with negatives—non-violence, non-compliance, non-betrayal. In such a time, friendship is reduced to the bone. It becomes a matter of non-betrayal. Stringfellow saw betrayal on all sides (as indeed all but the purblind must see)—the large betrayal of public trust, public monies, the public compact . . . What was manifestly impossible in public life he created and cherished up close . . . There could exist in such a world a community of non-betrayal, non-cooperation, non-surrender. It required that the members enter a covenant, say their prayers, gather and then scatter to their work and above all, the first of all, cherish one another . . . My encounter with this spirit of Stringfellow and his non-betraying friendship dates notoriously from 1970 and events that occurred up the road from this chapel. I was lifted from the home of Stringfellow and trundled off the Island into prison . . . But for those few days, Stringfellow's home was the only church I knew. It was the

9. See Daloisio, Mauk, and Rogers, eds., *Ambassadors.*

only safe place in the universe. And this was the aspect of Christ that this Christian kept opening before his friends. Christ was our friend, in such a world, in such a lifetime as ours, precisely because He does not betray. He keeps covenant, He keeps His Word, even with us, even when we break covenant, break our word, betray . . . For thousands of us, [Stringfellow] became the honored keeper and guardian of the Word of God, that is to say, a Christian who could be trusted to keep his word, which was God's Word made his own . . . And that Word he kept and guarded and cherished now keeps him. This is the way with the Word, which we name Christ. The covenant keeps us who keep the covenant.[10]

Long before, at a festival of hope during the 1968 Catonsville trial, Stringfellow—weak and frail with extreme illness—had climbed the pulpit to utter, by Dan's account, a single terse testimony: "Death shall have no dominion!" The congregation rose in a standing ovation.

In the wake of Dan's arrest, Stringfellow found himself taking recourse to the book of Acts, specifically the account of the arrest of the apostles for healing the disabled beggar and for preaching the resurrection. It was the latter that so caught his attention. He read it and read it. What can "resurrection from the dead" mean if it is cause for arrest and imprisonment? He employed this text in preaching to his hometown congregation in Northampton a sermon called "An Authority Over Death."

> The preaching of the resurrection, far from being politically in-nocuous, and the healing incidents, instead of being merely pri-vate, are profound, even cosmic, political acts. . . . I do not imply that Berrigan is engaged in some self-conscious imitation of Peter or John or any other of the earlier Christians; I simply mean that to proclaim the resurrection in word and act is an affront which the State cannot tolerate because the resurrection exposes the sub-servience of the State to death as the moral purpose of the society which the State purports to rule.[11]

Indeed. Daniel Berrigan enjoyed and exercised that very freedom. He wrote of it himself, virtually as an "ethic."

> Simply put, we long to taste that event, its thunders and quakes, its great yes. We want to test the resurrection in our bones. To see if we might live in hope, instead of in the *silva oscura*, the

---

10. D. Berrigan, "A Homiletical Afterword," in Wylie-Kellermann, ed., *Essential*, 231–34.

11. Stringfellow and Towne, *Suspect Tenderness*, 73, 74.

thicket of cultural despair, nuclear despair, a world of perpetual war. We want to taste the resurrection. May I say we have not been disappointed.[12]

The night of our conversation about death, there was not yet a plaque of Dan's design on the wall behind us, but there soon would be. In spring 1986, we moved Anthony's ashes and joined them with Bill's beside the stone wall of the cottage. The plaque was a terse testimony: "Near this house the remains of William Stringfellow and Anthony Towne await the resurrection, Alleluia."

Now Dan's remains in earth, like his remains in us, anticipate that same freedom.

---

12. D. Berrigan, "An Ethic of Resurrection," in *Testimony*, 225.

Burial Aside: A Celtic Passage

[My wife Jeanie and I were on the Island with Dan and friends to celebrate an anniversary of Bill Stringfellow's death and to receive an icon of Bill which a fellow Jesuit, Bill McNichols, had produced. As we had a camera crew on hand to do interviews toward a Stringfellow film, I asked Dan if he would tell the story, on the very spot, of his arrest by the FBI that ended his underground period. He was a little reluctant, but I pressed, promising I'd never ask such of him again. He assented and told the story in a light-hearted, almost comical way. That evening Jeanie and I had dinner with him at the cottage. We had previously heard him tell a burial tale, garnered on a trip to Ireland, which Jeanie now sought to record and publish in an issue of *The Witness*[13] devoted to grief. As the temperate summer night wore on, she produced a tape recorder. Dan looked to me and said, "When does never begin?" But he obliged with what follows.]

I have a story to tell about a ritual on Clare Island, which is off the west coast of Ireland. It was one of the most devastated areas during the famine of the nineteenth century.

The winters out there in the North Atlantic are very cruel and the worst tragedy is the loss of young fishermen who go out with their fathers and are lost in the great winter storms. This loss is compounded with the fact that there's a Celtic idea that the sea is in charge. Once someone is swept overboard, efforts to recover the person are minimal, because it's looked upon as a curse to try to draw someone out of the sea. And you risk further trouble.

A friend of mine, Patrick O'Brien, was a new priest and his first parishioner, the daughter of a shepherd who had died thirty years before, was taken very ill that first winter. The helicopter was unable to arrive to take her to the mainland. They had to risk the boat. He went over with her—in her very bad condition in a very primitive open boat. In the middle of the storm, he was swept overboard into the January waters. Because he was the priest, they labored to recover him. He ended up in the hospital with the dying woman. He had pneumonia and barely, barely recovered; she died.

He got back on the Island in time for the funeral. He was a new priest and he was very attentive to the pre-Christian Celtic ceremonies.

---

13. D. Berrigan, "A Celtic Passage."

So it happened like this. In the little house where her father had lived and then she had lived, they set up the box on two chairs between the hearth and the table. People gathered all through and outside the house. O'Brien celebrated the Eucharist at the kitchen table. At the end of it, he knew enough to know that his part was over. He just joined the other people in the congregation.

Two men came forward and they kicked over the chairs, one in the direction of the hearth and one in the direction of the table. (We were later informed this was so the ghost would not return either to the hearth or the table.) Then they picked up the box, which had been sealed, and proceeded outdoors. They were followed by the entourage of people around the cottage. Chanting, they paced out—three times—a Celtic rune, which means that they did not finish the circle. In the Book of Kells, the rune is always an incomplete circle which ends mysteriously in another round and eventually the circle is completed, but it's never one circle. It's more like a maze. This was so that the ghost does not return to the house.

Well, they proceeded upward to the cliffs, the priest in the background. When they got near the cliffs a few of the men went down on hands and knees and began to move into the underbrush which is similar to Block Island's—the Atlantic does not allow for great trees. Because the soil is so thin, they cannot bury the dead; they shove them into the underbrush and leave them there.

The Celtic custom is that the daughter is buried on top of the father and the son is buried on top of the mother. So two people went in and they cleared the grave of her father, the shepherd.

They signalled to the people waiting to shove the box in to follow. They came in and the priest was foremost, as he told me. When they tried to justify the box of the daughter, the boards of the father's box broke apart and he was revealed. They could see that his hands were incorrupt; they were folded as on the day of his funeral. The priest said that they were just as fresh as his own hands.

So there was great tumult. The word passed back about this miracle.

Patrick O'Brien, a new priest, was confronted with this incredible dilemma: What do we do now? Everybody was looking at him. And he said it in a kind of quasi-panic, "Close it down!" And so they did. They replaced the boards and they shoved the daughter's box on top of the father's box and they repaired back to the house for the funeral feast.

As he was listening to the conversation that was going around during the meal, my friend realized that these people were not really amazed that the hands were incorrupt. He heard that the shepherd had healed people and sheep. But their understanding of the incorruption finally came clear, when he heard them say, "Well, no wonder. He never took any money. He was poor like us."

Afterword

Kateri Boucher

As I PREPARE TO write, I am searching the little library in Detroit's Catholic Worker house—my living room—for books marked Berrigan that I may have missed. One thin, pale spine catches my eye: *The Raft is Not the Shore*, coauthored by Daniel Berrigan and Thich Nhat Hanh. I flip it open and the cover promptly falls off. That old? I chuckle. An implicit recommendation from Catholic Workers past, I guess.

I never got to meet or correspond with Dan, so stories and books (both worn and new) are all I've got to go on. It wasn't even until reading Bill's book that I realized I have Dan to thank (among many others) for this very home I sit in. Who knew, over forty years ago, that his brief stint at the University of Detroit would leave behind a budding community of peace and resistance, including this Catholic Worker house—itself now well-worn, too.

A fellow Detroit Worker, Bill was one of the first to introduce me to Dan's work. He spoke of Dan with such familiarity, and recounted his life with such "aliveness," that I felt I was indeed being introduced to Dan himself. As I write, I notice that I've even begun to refer to him simply as "Dan." This inherited familiarity is a testament, I think, to both Dan's life and Bill's loving witness to it.

Although I wish I could share a cup of tea with Dan, or a sip of scotch, I still feel invited to sit at this table with him. To break bread together. To *eat this book* and feast on these resurrected apples, presented here in deep-dish form. I arrive as an eager newcomer, relating to Dan as both an elder and an ancestor in this work.

Bill reflects:

> *and our once fresh formation*
> *turns, can it be, toward eldering.*

And I wonder: In the growing wake of his death, what does it mean for Dan to continue eldering us? What does it mean, as the next generation stepping into this world, to receive him as such? How do we look back on his life not as a "moral cipher" (as cautions Bill) but as a way of turning more fully to face the moment we are in?

And holy hell, what a moment this is. I'm sometimes tempted to call these times unprecedented, but I imagine Dan would caution otherwise. He was a biblical scholar, I remind myself. State violence, imperialism, pandemic . . . Which part, exactly, is new?

The depth of his rooting in the biblical tradition was rare in his day, and would be counted even more rare now. In most millennial activist spaces, the Bible isn't exactly popular fare. Many of us, myself included, have come to age with iPhones in hand, caught however accidentally in the capitalist obsession with the new, the young, the shiny—and consequently suspicious (or dismissive) of anything that whiffs of age. What does the Bible have to do with today's movements for liberation? Why root ourselves in a tradition so *ancient*? Not to mention so messy, so rife with contradiction?

For many years, I stayed away from the Bible, too uncertain in how to approach it and unconvinced that it held any value for me. But in the last few years, gently invited by Bill and other elders in the tradition, I began to slowly dip my toes into Bible studies, *lectio divina* circles, and seminary classes. Dan's work has animated my curiosity throughout. He insisted (can I say insists?) that this Big Old Book is not simply a historical relic, but a living, breathing document that can speak straight to our struggles today. *Who would have thought that meditating on Haggai or Zechariah during the Persian Gulf War* [insert current crisis here] *could preserve one's moral sanity? Indeed prove the very act of sanity? That is Berrigan's claim.* I've been compelled by this claim, and ever more grateful for it. Dan's encouragement has helped me engage more deeply with this text, messy as it may be, and find within it ongoing threads of resistance, resilience, and wisdom.

Beyond his biblical analysis, learning about Dan's own life has become for me a gospel study in and of itself. The way he practiced the works of mercy through hospice care, accompanying folks with AIDS, and visiting the imprisoned (sometimes in close quarters). His commitment to grounding in solitude and growing in community. Not to mention his many playful and prophetic pranks pulled on the state. As I navigate my own relationship with Christianity, I've been deeply moved by the way he read the Gospels with "life and death seriousness." But honestly? I've been just as moved by how much *joy* he brought to the whole thing: a reminder not to take myself too seriously, even amidst the struggle. I am one of many who has been "formed and transformed by immersion in his witness."

Of course, as with all elders I think, this relationship can be complicated. I resonated with Jeanie Wylie's experience at Block Island, and the "certain male ambiance of the monastic environs" that can permeate even these theologians' written work. I still wonder sometimes if their tradition is "for me," or if I even want it to be.

My friend Grace Aheron wrote about this very question for *Geez* magazine's issue on powers and principalities. A self-identified queer Asian American femme, seminary dropout, and organizer, Grace asked, "Do I want to inherit this theology?" At times, she said, she hasn't "wanted it near [her] at all—no matter how lefty" but these days she more often finds herself a "curious magpie," turning to the words of these theologians-gone-before and "holding them up to the light" of the present moment.

> When done on my own terms, this work is a practice of delight: cartwheeling into the solemn worlds of those I've termed the monk bros (—yes, I know they weren't all monks). I get to listen to these guys whom I really do treasure and respect, and then scamper off, grinning and excited, clutching their words to my chest. I know these actions bring honour and delight to them too—I imagine the Berrigans and Stringfellow and their friends looking from Glory at their books in my brown hands, long neon-painted fingernails, topless and tipsy on a queer beach in Queens . . . and they're laughing and shaking their heads in wonder at me, an unlikely heir.

This tradition is not just ours to blindly accept, but to be in conversation with. To ask questions of, to challenge. I don't necessarily feel called to model my life after Dan's specific actions, and I'm sure we would disagree on matters both theological and political. But I find resonance with the questions he relentlessly asked through his life, knowing that the answers of my generation will be—in fact, *need* to be—different than his own. We are "getting born and it's bloody. It's always bloody." But we can take comfort in knowing that we are not the first, and we are most certainly not alone.

Bill asks, "In a priestly lifetime, how many souls on this sweet and beset old planet has Berrigan called to life in the gospel?" I wonder if "lifetime" is too limiting a frame. How many people and communities around the world continue to feel the ripples of his presence? I surely feel his here today, still calling me and us to meet the moment we are in, uncertain as it is, and root ourselves firmly and joyfully in the promise of resurrection.

Decades ago, Dan wrote: *We were trying to live in the world as though we contained the future.* Perhaps this is why we feel his spirit so strong still; maybe he really has been here before, catching himself in the current of a stream that moves beyond space and time. I take comfort knowing his spirit may be waiting up ahead, too, urging us to move forward and pointing us to look back. I imagine my generation coming to him with our burning questions, our crises of the moment. "Dan, we are scared. There are worlds ending. We are dying." I can almost hear the wry response: "Gee, that must be exciting!"

Kateri Boucher was raised in a suburb of Rochester, New York, and became a full-time student of Detroit, Michigan (Waawiyatanong) in the fall of 2018. She is associate editor for Geez *magazine and a community member in Detroit's Catholic Worker house.*

Bibliography

Berrigan, Daniel. *Absurd Convictions, Modest Hopes: Conversations after Prison with Lee Lockwood*. New York: Vintage, 1973.

———. "All Honor to the Wrong People." *WIN Magazine*, vol. X, no. 11, March 28, 1974, 14–15.

———. *America is Hard to Find*. New York: Doubleday, 1972.

———. *Block Island*. Greensboro, NC: Unicorn, 1985.

———. "A Celtic Passage." *The Witness*, vol. 80, no. 3, March 1997, 18–19.

———. *Consequences, Truth, And . . .* New York: Macmillan, 1966.

———. "Covenant and Conquest." Reprinted as "The Middle East: Sane Conduct?" In *The Great Berrigan Debate*, 1–8. New York: The Committee on New Alternatives in the Middle East, January 1974.

———. "A Homiletical Afterword." In *William Stringfellow: Essential Writings*, edited by Bill Wylie-Kellermann, 231–34. Maryknoll, NY: Orbis, 2013.

———. "Killing for the Love of the Kingdom." *National Catholic Reporter*, May 5, 1978.

———. *Lights on in the House of the Dead*. New York: Doubleday, 1974.

———. *Minor Prophets, Major Themes*. Marion, SD: Fortcamp, 1995.

———. *The Mission: A Film Journal*. New York: Harper & Row, 1986.

———. "My Friend." In *Radical Christian and Exemplary Lawyer*, edited by Andrew W. McThenia, Jr., 96–102. Grand Rapids: Eerdmans, 1995.

———. *No Bars to Manhood*. Garden City, NY: Doubleday, 1970.

———. "Of Priests, Women, Women Priests, and Other Unlikely Recombinants: A Diary." In *Why Men Priests?*, edited by Mary Condren, 8–10. Dublin: SCM, 1977.

———. *Prison Poems*. New York: Viking, 1973.

———. *And the Risen Bread*. Edited by John Dear. New York: Fordham University Press, 1998.

———. *Ten Commandments for the Long Haul*. Nashville: Abingdon, 1981.

———. *Testimony*. Maryknoll, NY: Orbis, 2004.

———. *They Call Us Dead Men*. New York: Macmillan, 1966.

———. *Time Without Number*. New York: Macmillan, 1957.

———. *To Dwell In Peace: An Autobiography*. San Francisco: Harper & Row, 1987.

———. *The Trial of the Catonsville Nine*. Boston: Beacon, 1970.

———. *Vietnamese Letter*. New York: Thomas Merton Center/Hoa Binh, 1972.

———. *We Die Before We Live*. New York: Seabury, 1980.

Berrigan, Daniel, Hans Morgenthau, with John H. Hamilton. "The Fifty-first State," on WNET. Transcribed in *The Great Berrigan Debate*, 21–26. New York: Committee on Alternatives in the Middle East, January, 1974.

Berrigan, Daniel, and Thich Nhat Hanh. *The Raft Is Not the Shore: Conversations Toward a Buddhist/Christian Awareness*. Boston: Beacon, 1975.

Berrigan, Jerry. "Remembering his Uncle." *Radical Discipleship*, October 18, 2016. https://radicaldiscipleship.net/2016/20/18/remembering-his-uncle/.

Blitzer, Jonathan. "The Life and Death of Juan Sanabria, One of New York City's First Coronavirus Victims." *The New Yorker*, April 6, 2020. https://www.newyorker.com/news/postscript/the-life-and-death-of-juan-sanabria-one-of-new-york-citys-first-coronavirus-victims.

Bonhoeffer, Dietrich. *Letters and Papers from Prison*. Edited by Eberhard Bethge. Translated by Reginald Fuller. New York: Macmillan, 1957.

———. *Life Together*. New York: Harper & Row, 1954.

Camus, Albert. "Neither Victims Nor Executioners." In *Seeds of Liberation*, edited by Paul Goodman, 24–43. New York: George Braziller, 1964.

———. *The Plague*. Translated by Stuart Gilbert. New York: Vintage, 1991.

———. "The Unbeliever and the Christians." In *Resistance, Rebellion, and Death*, 69–74. New York: Vintage, 1974.

Cleaver, Eldridge. *Soul on Ice*. New York: Delta, 1968.

Cosacchi, Daniel, and Eric Martin, eds. *The Berrigan Letters: Personal Correspondence Between Daniel and Philip Berrigan*. Ossining, NY: Orbis, 2016.

Daloisio, Amanda, Dan Mauk, and Terry Rogers, eds. *Ambassadors of God: Selected Obituaries from The Catholic Worker*. Eugene, OR: Resource, 2018.

Day, Dorothy. *The Long Loneliness*. New York: Harper and Row, 1952.

de Antonio, Emile, dir. *In the King of Prussia*. Turin Film, 1982.

———. *In the Year of the Pig*. Turin Film, 1969.

Dear, John. *The Sacrament of Civil Disobedience*. Baltimore: Fortkamp, 1994.

Dear, John, ed. *Apostle of Peace*. Maryknoll, NY: Orbis,1996.

———. *Daniel Berrigan: Essential Writings*. Maryknoll, NY: Orbis, 2009.

Douglass, James. "The Converging Martyrdom of Malcolm and Martin." Dr. Martin Luther King Jr. Lecture, Princeton Theological Seminary, March 29, 2006.

———. *Gandhi and the Unspeakable: His Final Experiment with Truth*. Maryknoll, NY: Orbis, 2012.

———. *JFK and the Unspeakable: Why He Died and Why it Matters*. Maryknoll, NY: Orbis, 2008.

Forest, Jim. *At Play in the Lion's Den*. Maryknoll, NY: Orbis, 2017.

———. *The Root of War is Fear*. Maryknoll, NY: Orbis, 2016.

Forest, Jim, ed. "Contemplation and Resistance: A Conversation Between Nhat Hanh and Daniel Berrigan." *WIN Magazine*, vol. IX, no. 17, June 4, 1973, 4–10.

Ginsberg, Allen. "Yaweh and Allah Battle." *WIN Magazine*, vol. X, no. 11, March 28, 1974, 12–13.

Hagadorn, Sue, dir. *Seeking Shelter: A Story of Faith, Place, and Resistance*. New York: Seedworks Film Foundation, 2018.

Hagadorn, Sue, the Reale Brothers, and Richard Dresser, dirs. *The Berrigans: Devout and Dangerous*. New York: Seedworks Film Foundation, 2021.

Hallie, Phillip. *Lest Innocent Blood Be Shed*. New York: Harper & Row, 1979.

Harding, Vincent. "Foreword." In *Jesus and the Disinherited*, by Howard Thurman, vii–xviii. Boston: Beacon, 1996.

Heschel, Abraham. *The Prophets: An Introduction*. New York: Harper, 1969.

Joffe, Roland, dir. *The Mission*. New York: Goldcrest Films; Burbank, CA: Warner Bros., 1986.

Kelly, Stephen. "Do Not Be Ruled by Fear, But by Faith." *Sojourners*, August 2016, 20.

King, Martin Luther, Jr. "A Time to Break Silence." In *A Testament of Hope: The Essential Writings and Speeches of Martin Luther King, Jr.*, edited by James M. Washington, 233–34. San Francisco: Harper & Row, 1986.

———. "Letter from a Birmingham Jail." In *A Testament of Hope: The Essential Writings and Speeches of Martin Luther King, Jr.*, edited by James M. Washington, 289–302. San Francisco: Harper & Row, 1986.

Kirk-Duggan, Cheryl A. *Exorcising Evil: A Womanist Perspective on the Spirituals*. Maryknoll, NY: Orbis, 1997.

Laffin, Art. *Swords into Plowshares: A Chronology*. Marion, SD: Rose Hill, 2003.

Lockwood, Lee, dir. *Holy Outlaw*. National Educational Television, 1970.

Martin, Eric. "A Theology of Disobedience: The Conversion of Daniel Berrigan 1953–1966." PhD diss., Fordham University, NY, June 2019.

Merton, Thomas. *Conjectures of a Guilty Bystander*. Garden City, NY: Image, 1968.

———. *Selected Poems of Thomas Merton*. New York: New Directions, 1967.

Merton, Thomas, ed. *The Wisdom of the Desert*. New York: New Directions, 1960.

Myers, Ched. *Binding the Strongman*. Maryknoll, NY: Orbis, 1988.

Nhat Hanh, Thich, and Vo-Dinh. *The Cry of Vietnam*. Santa Barbara, CA: Unicorn, 1971.

Oyer, Gordon. *Pursuing the Spiritual Roots of Protest*. Eugene, OR: Cascade, 2014.

Petiepierre, Dom Robert, OSB, ed. *Exorcism: The Findings of a Commission Convened by the Bishop of Exeter*. London: SPCK, 1972.

Polner, Murray, and Jim O'Grady. *Disarmed and Dangerous: The Radical Lives and Times of Philip and Daniel Berrigan*. New York: Basic, 1997.

Sachs, Lynne, dir. *Investigation of a Flame: A Portrait of the Catonsville Nine*. Brooklyn, NY: Icarus Films, 2003.

Stringfellow, William. *An Ethic for Christians and Other Aliens in a Strange Land*. Waco, TX: Word, 1973.

———. "Introduction." In *They Call Us Dead Men*. New York: Macmillan, 1966.

———. *A Second Birthday*. Garden City, NY: Doubleday, 1970.

———. *A Simplicity of Faith: My Experience in Mourning*. Nashville: Abingdon, 1982.

Stringfellow, William, and Anthony Towne. *Suspect Tenderness: The Ethics of the Berrigan Witness*. New York: Holt, Rinehart and Winston, 1971.

———. "A Statement by the Accused." In *Suspect Tenderness: The Ethics of the Berrigan Witness*, 120–22. New York: Holt, Rinehart and Winston, 1971.

Tropea, Joe, and Skizz Cyzyk, dirs. *Hit and Stay*. Baltimore: Haricot Vert Films, 2013.

Wills, Garry. "Modern Prophets?" *The Sun*, Baltimore, March 11, 1978.

Wylie-Kellermann, Bill. "Daniel Berrigan, Poetry Incarnate." *Geez* 53 (2019) 12–15.

———. "Death Shall Have No Dominion: Daniel Berrigan of the Resurrection." *Cross Currents*, vol. 66, no. 3, Fall 2016, 312–20.

———. *Dying Well: The Resurrected Life of Jeanie Wylie-Kellermann*. Detroit: Cass Community, 2018.

———. "Eucharist at Gunpoint." *Geez* 56 (2020) 25–27.

———. "The Politics of Friendship: Daniel Berrigan and William Stringfellow." Transcription of a talk at Loyola University Chicago sponsored by the Hank Center for the Catholic Intellectual Heritage, during "Berrigan Week," 2019.

———. *Principalities in Particular: A Practical Theology of the Powers That Be.* Minneapolis: Fortress, 2017.

———. Review of *The Berrigan Letters,* edited by Daniel Cosacchi and Eric Martin. *The Catholic Worker.* October–November 2016, 4.

———. "Review of *The Plague* by Albert Camus." *The Catholic Worker,* October–November (2020) 4–5.

———. *Seasons of Faith and Conscience: Reflections on Liturgical Direct Action.* Maryknoll, NY: Orbis, 1991. Republication Eugene, OR: Wipf & Stock, 2008.

———. "Taking the Book with Life and Death Seriousness." In *Apostle of Peace: Essays in Honor of Daniel Berrigan,* edited by John Dear, 87–91. Maryknoll, NY: Orbis, 1996.

———. "An Unbound Spirit: Review of *At Play in the Lion's Den* by Jim Forest." *Sojourners,* November 2018, 42–43.

———. "Words Can't Make it Happen." Transcription of a performance for Secret Society of Twisted Storytellers, March 21, 2014. Charles Wright Museum of African American History, Detroit.

Wylie-Kellermann, Bill, ed. *A Keeper of the Word: Selected Writings of William Stringfellow.* Grand Rapids: Eerdmans, 1994.

———. *William Stringfellow: Essential Writings.* Maryknoll, NY: Orbis, 2013.

Zaretsky, Robert. "Out of a Clear Blue Sky." *Times Literary Supplement,* April 10, 2020. https://www.the-tls.co.uk/articles-albert-camus-the-plague-coronavirus-essay-robert-zaretsky/.

Author Page

Bill Wylie-Kellermann is a non-violent community activist and United Methodist pastor retired from St. Peter's Episcopal Church Detroit. He is connected to the Detroit Catholic Worker and its soup kitchen, Manna Community Meal. In addition to *Celebrant's Flame,* he has authored six other books. Bill is co-founder of Word and World: A Peoples' School and adjunct faculty at Ecumenical Theological Seminary. A 1975 graduate of Union Theological Seminary in NYC, where he first met Berrigan, he has been engaged in direct action for justice and peace for five decades. His most recent trials and jailtime have come as part of the Homrich 9, prosecuted for blocking water shut-off trucks, and for actions with the Michigan Poor People's Campaign. Presently, he is involved in Detroit movement work concerning police brutality, the water struggle, and community-based research. He is married to Denise Griebler. In Jesus, he bets his life on gospel non-violence, good news to the poor, Word made flesh, and freedom from the power of death.

Other Books by Bill Wylie-Kellermann

Seasons of Faith and Conscience: Reflections on Liturgical Direct Action, (Maryknoll, NY: Orbis Books, 1991; Second Edition -Eugene OR: Wipf and Stock, 2008)

A Keeper of the Word: Selected Writings of William Stringfellow (Grand Rapids: Eerdmans, 1994)

William Stringfellow: Essential Writings, (Maryknoll, NY: Orbis Books, 2013)

Where the Waters Go Around: Beloved Detroit (Eugene OR: Cascade Books, 2017)

Principalities in Particular: A Practical Theology of the Powers that Be (Minneapolis, MN: Fortress Press, 2017)

Dying Well: The Resurrected Life of Jeanie Wylie-Kellermann (Detroit: Cass Community Publishing, 2018)

Index

CPSIA information can be obtained
at www.ICGtesting.com
Printed in the USA
FSHW010624240421
80636FS